W9-DIM-500

WITHDRAWN FROM LIBRARY

MONTGOMERY COLLEGE LIBRARY
ROCKVILLE CAMPUS

▶▶▶▶▶▶ Cinema One

1 Jean-Luc Godard

Jean-Luc Godard

Richard Roud

Indiana University Press
Bloomington and London

The Cinema One series is published by
Indiana University Press
in association with *Sight and Sound*
and the Education Department of the
British Film Institute

First United States publication 1967
Second revised edition published 1970

Library of Congress catalog card number: LC 70–115456
ISBN 0 253 13200 2 clothbound
ISBN 0 253 13201 0 paperbound

All rights reserved

No part of this book may be reproduced or utilized in any
form or by any means, electronic or mechanical, including
photocopying and recording, or by any information storage
and retrieval system, without permission in writing from
the publisher. The Association of American University
Presses Resolution on Permissions constitutes the only
exception to this prohibition

Printed in Great Britain

Contents

Godard in New York, 1968, shooting *1 A.M.*   *frontispiece*
(photograph by Kate Taylor)

Introduction   *page* 7

1 The Outsider   16

2 Politics   36

3 Narration   47

4 Reality and Abstraction   71

5 France, American style   101

6 *La Chinoise* and After: The Damascus Road   131

Appendix: Shorts and Sketches   154

Filmography   172

Cover: Juliet Berto in *La Chinoise*

Introduction

Jean-Luc Godard is, of all contemporary directors, the most controversial. For many, he is the most important film-maker of his generation; for others, he is, if not the worst, then the móst unbearable. However, as is often the case with controversial figures, he is admired and detested for the very same reasons. So it seems all the more important that a book about his work should seek essentially to describe and analyse, rather than to praise or criticise. One cannot hope to convince his detractors; on the contrary, a book which tries to explain Godard's aims and methods may well only confirm their objections: they will learn more exactly what it is they object to. No matter; it is to the others who, like myself, believe Godard to be not only the greatest director working in the cinema today (with the possible exception of Alain Resnais), but also one of the most important artists of our time, that this book is addressed.

Anyone who has given much thought to Godard's films has noticed their many contradictory elements, their paradoxes and abrupt alternations. "The subject of *Une Femme est une Femme*," he wrote, "is a character who succeeds in resolving a certain situation, but I conceived this subject within the framework of a neo-realistic musical: an *absolute contradiction*, but that is precisely why I wanted to make the film." Jean Collet, who wrote the first book on Godard,* actually concluded that the very key to his

* Jean Collet, *Jean-Luc Godard*, Editions Seghers, Paris, 1963.

Anna Karina and Jean-Luc Godard

work lay in his dialectical play between documentary and fiction. As Godard himself wrote: "Beauty and truth have two poles: documentary and fiction. You can start with either one. My starting-point is documentary to which I try to give the truth of fiction. That's why I've always worked with professional actors." In one of the very first articles he ever wrote (1950), Godard praised a Russian film because "it oscillated constantly between two poles, its heart-beat swinging back and forth from absolutes to action." So Godard has always been very much aware of his tendency to alternation, but contrary to Collet, I believe that the "play between documentary and fiction" is only one of the many dialectical elements that characterise his films.

Let us, however, consider for a moment the whole concept of dialectics, because it is one which is both central to Godard's work, and may be generally unfamiliar to Anglo-Saxon readers in anything other than its Marxist definition. At this point, too, one should note that French film directors—and writers, and artists—have always been more concerned with aesthetics and with philosophical problems in general than have the largely empirical Anglo-Saxons. This is in no way a value-judgment, simply a statement of a general tendency to which Godard is no exception. A case could, in fact, be made out for Godard having been strongly influenced by Hegelian ideas. But, just as Vico was not for James Joyce a philosopher in whom he 'believed', but rather an author who stimulated his imagination, who opened up new horizons, so Godard is not 'the perfect Hegelian' but rather an artist who has been influenced, directly or indirectly, by Hegelian notions.

Partly indirectly: as a child of his time—born in 1930, educated at the Sorbonne in the late 1940s—he could not but be influenced by the philosophical currents of the period, especially given the traditionally much greater interest in philosophical problems that the French have always shown. And the late 1940s in Paris was, of course, the heyday of Existentialism, of Sartre and Merleau-Ponty, both of whom were formed by Hegelian philosophy. There have been signs recently of a renewal of interest in Hegel in both England and America ("partly because of the impact on English and American philosophy of Sartre and Marx and partly because of Wittgenstein's demolition of traditional empiricist dogmas," said Martin Milligan in a recent review of a new edition of Hegel). In France he has never been forgotten, and an Existentialist like Merleau-Ponty went so far as to declare that Hegel "was at the origin of all that has been great in philosophy since the nineteenth century." And in one of Godard's first shorts, *Tous les Garçons s'appellent Patrick*, one of the girls, a student at the Sorbonne, is shown quite naturally clutching to her bosom a paperback copy of Hegel's *Aesthetics*. (The same book makes a reappearance, by the way, in *Une Femme est une Femme*.)

What is this connection, then, between Hegel and Godard? One of Hegel's most important concepts was that contradictions are the source of all movement and indeed of all life. "All things," said Hegel, "are in themselves contradictory, and it is this principle, more than any other, which expresses the truth, the very essence of things." If an idea calls up its opposite, this must mean that each concept is but a one-sided abstraction. Therefore an idea can only be completed by its contrary. Which is why Godard once said "Truth is in all things, even, partly, in error," and why Brice Parain—in *Vivre sa Vie*—goes even further to state that "Error is necessary to truth."

"I believe in dialectics," said Godard; and there are several reasons why this principle, this method of thought, might appeal to him. Of course, it was, as I said, in the air. And one could add that a philosopher like Merleau-Ponty thought that Existentialist philosophy and the cinema both had in common a certain way of being, a certain view of the world which was that of the generation who discovered both the cinema and Existentialism just after the Second World War. Another link between the cinema and Existentialism is that both are more interested in the actions, the behaviour, of men than in their thoughts.

But of course the cinema itself has always been the most paradoxical, the most contradictory of all the arts in its very essence. It is at once a narrative and a visual art, and from the very beginning there have been some film-makers who were interested in

9

telling stories, and others who were more preoccupied with visual and formal beauty.

There exists another, even more basic paradox in the art of the cinema. The movie camera was invented as a means of mechanically and accurately reproducing reality. The Lumière brothers, for example, used it for that, and that alone—or at least that is what they *thought* they were doing. Just as often, however, the camera has been used for a totally different purpose: Méliès did not try to reproduce reality, he often tried to re-create fantasy. Most fiction films are made by placing in front of a mechanical means of reproduction—the camera—people who are costumed, made-up, and trained to pretend they are something different from what they really are. (Macha Méril tells us that on *Une Femme Mariée* Godard was very much aware of this paradox, and in some scenes he wrote her dialogue; in others she was obliged to improvise; and in still others he used a tiny microphone, which she wore behind her ear, to ask questions which would prompt certain responses from her. And Godard himself has told us that although in the early films Anna Karina improvised almost all her dialogue, in the later ones she learned how to pretend she was improvising.)

So one could say that the whole art of the cinema rests on three polarities, three contradictions, three paradoxes: visual versus narrative, fiction versus documentary, and perhaps most important, reality versus abstraction. Godard, of course, is not the first director to have been aware of these contradictions. A director like Feuillade, consciously or unconsciously, derived much of the strength of his melodramatic fiction films from his use of naked filmed reality. And a director like von Sternberg was certainly aware of the demands of abstraction: reduced to their narrative interest or their documentary value, most of his films would cease to exist.

But Godard seems more alive than most directors to these contradictions; in fact, I think he has chosen to build his films on them. Like Hegel, he has decided that truth and beauty lie, not in either alternative, nor yet in a synthesis of the two, but rather in a conscious exploitation of these seeming contradictions. "The camera," he wrote, "is not only a reproducing apparatus; the cinema is not an art which films life: the cinema is something *between* art and life. Unlike painting and literature, the cinema both gives to life and takes from it, and I try to render this concept in my films. Literature and painting both exist as art from the very start; the cinema doesn't."

There are many polarities in Godard's films—his alternation between a romantic view of life and a naturalistic one, between psychological motivation and pure chance, between the use of stars and non-stars—but there are three which seem to me to be capital. First, there is the contrast in his work between personal and social preoccupations. A question of content more than of form, perhaps, but the distinction between the two is not really valid in the case of Godard. "To me," he said, "style is just the outside of content, and content the inside of style, like the outside and the inside of the human body—both go together, they can't be separated." However, it is true that Godard has completely revised conventional notions of content. Occasionally form itself can be the content of a film, or content can be form—at least a subject is chosen because of its formal possibilities. Much of twentieth-century art has retreated from content. Monet's water-lilies are not the real subject of his *Nymphéas*: he presumably chose to paint them because they made possible certain experiments in colour and pattern. Godard, on the other hand, neither rejects nor embraces content, as such; he has succeeded in keeping content and form in a kind of perpetual balance. The one does not 'express' the other; each, so to speak, expresses itself. And this, I suggest, is because he has realised, as has no other director, the paradoxical nature of film aesthetics.

There is also a constant swing in Godard's work between the imperatives of narrative and those of comment: novel versus essay. Godard has even revolutionised the very idea of narration. As a corollary, there is also a perpetual contrast between movement and stasis: an ever-changing balance between his use of brief takes and long ones, and the building up of these takes into sequences of varying length.

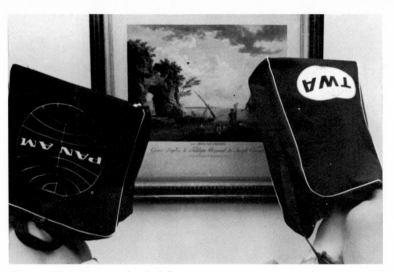

Deux ou Trois Choses que je sais d'elle

Most important of all, I think, is Godard's solution to the problem of the alternate claims of reality and abstraction. The success with which he has resolved this problem makes him for me the most 'advanced' of all directors—in so far as one can ever conceive of the idea of progress in the arts. His last two films to date,* *Made in U.S.A.* and *Deux ou Trois Choses que je sais d'elle*, deserve detailed consideration because in this respect both represent peaks in Godard's career: the former pushes to extreme limits certain forms of experimentation, the latter successfully consolidates them.

---

* This introduction and the five chapters that follow were written and published in 1967. Since that jubilee year, Godard's career has taken such a Big Leap that, rather than revise with 20-20 hindsight and a posteriori insight, it seemed wiser to write about *La Chinoise* and After separately. All the more so since *La Chinoise* marked a new beginning, a radical attempt 'to start from zero'.

R.R., January 1970

15

Chapter One

More, perhaps, than in the work of any other director, Godard's subjects and themes are rooted in the world in which they are set; or conversely, perhaps, their setting has conditioned the choice of themes. Godard's world is a very special one: it is urban, transient, grey. In his films the country is simply a space you have to go through to get to another city. The one important exception to this rule is the idyll on the island of Porquerolles in *Pierrot le Fou*, but of course it is just that—an idyll, and one which, given his other films, one knew to be doomed. And so it was.

His City is Paris, and it is the Paris of hotel rooms, *chambres de bonnes*, and, above all, cafés, with their pin-ball machines and the endless conversations nursing the *lait chaud* against the inevitable moment when one has to go out on the streets or back to the dreary hotel room. So one drinks, and eats, and talks; one stands at the bar or sits down at a table. No one in his films has a flat, a home. Or if they do, they have either just moved in or are just about to move out. In *Le Mépris* the Roman flat of Camille and Paul has got barely a few sticks of furniture, no curtains, no carpets. In the flat to which Marianne Renoir takes Ferdinand/Pierrot, there is hardly any furniture—just a divan-bed in a corner. *Une Femme est une Femme* has the most solidly furnished apartment of them all, but even there one feels that Angéla and Emile could move out to-morrow, leaving no trace behind—nor would they want to leave any signs of their passing. His characters are nomadic in every

sense; one oasis looks like any other; all are equally indifferent, equally transitory.

Nature is present only in that obscene parody of it, the suburbs, as in *Bande à Part* with its long dreary avenues, its canals and rivers, its empty lots where no tree ever blossoms. Even more depressing is the locale of *Les Carabiniers*—the *zone*, that dreary *terrain vague* that encircles Paris, with its corrugated-iron huts and its pitiful scrub.

No, Paris is his world, and it is the Paris of the outsiders. Foreigners, gangsters, prostitutes, students: all those on the fringes of society in any city, and made to feel even more so in what Godard finds at its height in Paris, the crushing presence of a bourgeois society. A *bande à part*, a group of outsiders, even though Godard paradoxically claimed that it is the world which is the outsider; his characters represent life; the world is just a bad movie.

In this urban society, the underground, the overhead railway, the peripheral boulevards, the arcades and passageways play an important part. Particularly the overhead railway, which cuts through Paris, and at the same time bears down heavily upon it—of the city, but not part of it. He even uses a shot of the *métro aérien* in *Bande à Part* to symbolise the doom which is awaiting his characters, their inescapable fatality. Passageways, such as in *A Bout de Souffle*, and arcades, as in *Masculin Féminin*, represent the secret ways his exiles get around the great ant-hill, privileged corridors which avoid the menacing streets.

Hardly any of his characters seem to have families. No fathers, mothers, brothers, sisters. Occasionally an uncle or an aunt, as in *Bande à Part*, and then not very much imbued with family feeling. Many of his characters are literally outsiders, foreigners: Jean Seberg in *A Bout de Souffle* and *Le Grand Escroc*; Anna Karina throughout; Marina Vlady in *Deux ou Trois Choses que je sais d'elle*; Laszlo Szabo, etc. Resnais once said jokingly that the only element linking all his films is the presence of at least one actor speaking with an accent, and Godard might well say the same. Godard has advanced another, purely formal reason for his continued use of

accents: "I like people, especially women, who speak French with a foreign accent. It's always rather pretty, and it gives to ordinary words a certain freshness and value that they normally have lost."

Occasionally this grim world is lit up by a kind of urban epiphany, a moment or two of pure joy, or, as he puts it, "a nostalgic moment of spontaneous gaiety and simplicity," such as the scene where Anna Karina, Sami Frey, and Claude Brasseur do an impromptu Madison in a café at the gates of Paris, or even Anna Karina's 'mating dance' in the billiard-room of *Vivre sa Vie*. Occasionally there are moments of tenderness, and of friendship, but not often. Otherwise, Paris is Eluard's *Capitale de la Douleur*, and that is why one was not surprised when Godard chose to shoot *Alphaville* there: Alphaville, nightmare city of the future in the Paris of today. The sense of menace was already there for Godard, and the pain, too.

However depressing this world may seem, Godard has nevertheless penetrated its beauty as well. Indeed, his whole aesthetic is based on finding the paradoxical beauty of these squalid surroundings. His world may be grey, but within this greyness he and his faithful cameraman, Raoul Coutard, have found an almost inexhaustible spectrum of colour. From this architectural poverty, they have created, or rather found, the beauty of bare walls, curtainless windows, and garish neon-lit cafés. It is a very modern, austere kind of beauty which does not depend upon 'art direction', but rather on an almost puritanical study of form. Even windowframes and handles can look like monumental sculpture, Godard seems to be saying, if one looks at them with a fresh and unprejudiced eye.

A parenthesis: I prefer Godard's films in black and white for this very reason. To be sure, the colour in *Une Femme est une Femme*, *Le Mépris*, and *Pierrot le Fou* is beautiful, but it somehow seems an easier kind of beauty, and one which others have also achieved. His last two colour films, *Made in U.S.A.* and *Deux ou Trois Choses que je sais d'elle*, are rather more special cases, as we shall see.

Therefore, considering the world in which Godard's films are set, it should come as no surprise that his main, all-penetrating

← *Bande à Part:* The Madison (Claude Brasseur, Anna Karina, Sami Frey)

theme is the impossibility of love, the impossibility of it lasting. ("Et réciproquement," as his characters never tire of saying; perhaps the choice—in so far as there is a conscious *choice*—of theme dictated the settings.) Almost without exception, this theme is present in each of his films. Sometimes a relationship is destroyed by cowardice, as in *A Bout de Souffle*; sometimes by political considerations, as in *Le Petit Soldat*, and partly in *Pierrot le Fou*. But most often it is simply life, the human condition. Not social conditions, however, although they do play some part in *Vivre sa Vie*, *Bande à Part*, and *Deux ou Trois Choses que je sais d'elle*. Nor is it Godard's much talked of misogyny for, after all, his female characters are just as often the victims.

However, it should be said that there *is* always a victim: the couples are never equal in strength. One is weak, the other strong, either basically or momentarily. In *Masculin Féminin*, Paul and Madeleine are united by physical bonds alone, and these prove to be insufficient—in any case, it is clear that Paul is much more in love than is Madeleine. In *Le Mépris*, it is perhaps Paul's cowardice that leads Camille to despise him, although we never really know why their marriage breaks up, except that perhaps it was never a true marriage in the first place. In *Made in U.S.A.* Paula, while trying to avenge her lover's death, discovers that it may have been caused by a sordid affair with a girl; political considerations may have played little part.

There are four apparent exceptions to this rule: *Une Femme est une Femme*, *Alphaville*, *Bande à Part*, and *Les Carabiniers*. In the first three, the relationship is saved at the end of the film by a stylistic pirouette which carries little conviction. To be sure, Lemmy Caution takes Natacha away from Alphaville and she learns to pronounce the forbidden words "I love you", but one has little confidence in this happy end. The machines would really have won out, just as, Godard would say, they actually are winning already. *Une Femme est une Femme* really *is* an exception, except that one cannot take very seriously the affair between Angéla and Emile. Only in *Les Carabiniers* do we find two happily married couples, but they are on such a low social and intellectual level that

25

Godard might well be saying that it is only on this brutish level that love can survive, that between ordinarily intelligent people it is doomed.

However, as I have suggested, the themes of Godard's films are alternatively and simultaneously both personal and social, and in order to examine fully the personal themes, one must also take into account the social aspects of his work. His films are both essay and diary, and one cannot be separated from the other. And, indeed, we discover that the purely personal themes tend to be subsumed and absorbed by the social ones.

For example, a very important theme, and one that comes up over and over again, is that of prostitution—a subject which is both personal and social at the same time. The treatment of prostitution begins on the personal level and slowly spreads, or rather enlarges itself, to take in social considerations as well. Or perhaps Godard simply discovered that the two are inseparable, as in fact they are. The tightest bond which links any of us to the social structure is what the Marxists call the cash nexus. We all have to eat, and to earn money in order to do so. And one of Godard's main contentions is that many of us earn that money by doing things we don't want to do. "More and more the people I see, and I meet many different kinds in the film milieu (one comes into contact with every level of society when one makes films, from the banker to the electrician), don't really enjoy what they're doing. Like prostitutes, they just do it. All they really want is a car to take them to the seaside. Except that when they get the car there won't be enough roads to get to the sea, and if they do, the beaches will be too crowded. I don't think," he adds, "that you can find a single carpenter or plumber today who likes his job." There may be a certain naïveté in these ideas, which we will consider later in discussing his most recent film, but they are obviously deeply felt.

In *Vivre sa Vie, Deux ou Trois Choses que je sais d'elle*, and in his sketch *L'An 2,000* in the episode film *L'Amour à travers les Ages*, Godard deals with prostitution in its most literal form: women selling their bodies. Nana, heroine of *Vivre sa Vie*, is left in the

Vivre sa Vie: one of the scenes cut by British censors

Deux ou Trois Choses que je sais d'elle: Marina Vlady and client

Le Mépris: Jack Palance and Brigitte Bardot

lurch by her husband: her baby farmed out, harassed by debts, she slowly slips into prostitution as a means of survival. Only to find it difficult (and, in her case, impossible) to get out. In the other two films prostitution is treated more complexly, as a part of—or perhaps a symbol for—a more general form of selling one's self.

The first hint of Godard's interest in the subject came in the light-hearted *Une Femme est une Femme.* In that film Angéla also sells her body; only as a strip-tease artist, to be sure, but the implications are clear, or at least they become so retrospectively. In *Le Mépris,* Godard goes on to a more complex form of prostitution. Michel Piccoli plays a writer who is mainly interested in the theatre but who lets himself be hired by a Hollywood producer to collaborate on the scripting of *The Odyssey* for a super-spectacle film. He has already written one script, *Toto versus Hercules,* but this was 'only' pure prostitution: *The Odyssey* will be a more complex case because here his real talents as a writer will be required, paid for, and degraded. And in becoming a prostitute he will in some obscure way lose his manhood.

Unlike Nana, he does not really need the money; he thinks it will allow him a better standard of living, and that by being able to pay off his expensive flat, he will be able to secure more strongly his wife's affections. The contrary, of course, turns out to be true, and her contempt for him is related to his selling himself to the producer. So when she allows the producer to make love to her, her never-formulated excuse might well be that if her husband can sell his brain to this man, she might as well—or even, is morally bound to—hand over the use of her body. Which can be taken as a growing realisation on Godard's part that the personal and the social are inextricably intertwined.

The theme of prostitution is further enlarged in this film when Lang quotes the famous Brecht poem written in Hollywood: "Each morning I go into the marketplace to sell my wares. . . ." For the cinema is not only the dream factory, it is also the great intellectual whorehouse; in recent years it has been overtaken by the advertising industry, but for many years it reigned supreme. (Think of Fitzgerald and the others who sold themselves for large scented swimming-pools, and wept bitter tears into them.)

Une Femme Mariée takes up a different and still more complex form of prostitution, the condition of marriage. The heroine, the film makes abundantly clear (and so did the original title: *La Femme Mariée*), is an object. An object for her husband, an object to take care of their child, to keep the house going, to have sex with. Hence a view of marriage as a kind of legalised prostitution, or as Kant put it, as a contract assuring the signatories the exclusive use of each other's sexual organs. Her relation to her lover is never made clear, perhaps because neither she nor he knows what it is. *Les Carabiniers* was Godard's first attack on the advertising world (to kill for a Maserati, to go to war for a *brassière Rosy* or a *slip Raoul*), but here he really takes on the problem: "The woman in *Une Femme Mariée*," he said, "is in fact already an inhabitant of Alphaville—woman reduced to an object by the pressures of modern life, incapable of being herself." But she is also an object that consumes, and throughout the film she is confronted with posters, handouts, all urging her to buy this, to do that. She is told how to measure her bust, and if it doesn't come up to industrial norms, how to make it bigger; how to be sexy, how to be desirable: in other words, how to increase her value on the open market.

In *Pierrot le Fou* Godard will touch on the world of the advertisers themselves: the cocktail-party to which Ferdinand is dragged by his wife where all the guests talk in slogans. And one of the reasons Ferdinand flees his comfortable flat and his rich wife is because she is trying to persuade him to prostitute himself, to get a job in advertising. Here in *Une Femme Mariée* he is concerned only with the receiving end, but this is also a form of prostitution, or rather the pre-conditioning for it. Advertising makes people want more than they have, and thus obliges them to prostitute themselves to buy the things others are prostituting themselves to sell to them: the eternal vicious circle of the consumer society. "I think that advertising is prostitution; it's pimping. I call a prostitute anyone who does something he doesn't want to. If I worked in advertising [actually Godard did work in the publicity department of Twentieth Century-Fox for a while] or if I worked for Simca and all day long I said nice things about Simcas even though I really preferred Ferraris, then I would be prostituting myself to Simca."

In *Alphaville*, prostitution is regimented by the State, and there are licensed seducers, first, second, and third class. But the whole city and its inhabitants have prostituted themselves to an idea of efficiency and progress, to the computer. Everything else must be sacrificed—most of all, love and tenderness—to this effective running of the State. Hence the need for State-licensed prostitutes and State-supplied tranquillisers. However, the relation between advertising and Alphaville is also quite clear. In the words of Marshall McLuhan: "To put the matter abruptly, the advertising industry is a crude attempt to extend the principles of automation to every aspect of society. Ideally, advertising aims at the goal of a programmed harmony among all human impulses and aspirations and endeavours. Using handicraft methods, it stretches out toward the ultimate electronic goal of a collective consciousness. When all production and all consumption are brought into a pre-established harmony with all desire and all effort, then advertising will have liquidated itself by its own success." In other words: Alphaville.

In *Masculin Féminin* there are fewer references to literal prostitution, but it is significant that Paul and his friends often discuss the matter. And here the more personal side of the subject returns, perhaps the misogynistic side. Since Paul is unable to achieve any intellectual *rapport* with Madeleine, since their interests are so widely divergent, and since the girls are more conditioned by consumer society and its publicists—more the daughters of Coca-Cola than of Marx—then, Godard seems to be asking, cannot the answer to Paul's sexual needs be better found in the occasional fling with the prostitute? She will give him with much less fuss what Madeleine can give, what she can only give.

But in *Masculin Féminin* Godard begins the final expansion of the theme of prostitution to the national and even international level. For the daughters of Coca-Cola represent the way in which much of the world has prostituted itself to American ideals, and, in many cases, to America itself. This might sound like a bit of Gaullist anti-American propaganda, but in his last two films we will see that this is not so. For Godard takes on the French government there as well. When he appeared on a television programme on the State-controlled network, he pretended to be surprised at the astonishment of another speaker on seeing a prostitute on a television programme: "But one sees them on TV day in and day out," said Godard. The government, he continued, uses an advertising agency. That is to say, it sells men like objects, as if the most important thing about politics was how to package the product rather than to institute a kind of dialogue, a discussion. That, he added, is why people like prostitutes so much—you don't have to talk to them in order to make love, and this is really serious, because love should be, above all, a kind of dialogue.

Therefore, if he chose to take up again the problem of prostitution in *Deux ou Trois Choses que je sais d'elle*, it is because, he said, "It seems to me that in and around Paris today, we are all living more or less in a state of prostitution. The increase in prostitution, literally speaking, is a partial proof of this statement because it calls into question the body, but one can prostitute oneself just as well with the mind, the spirit. I think it is a collective phenomenon, and perhaps one which is not altogether new. But what *is* new is that people now find it normal."

Une Femme Mariée: Macha Méril. How far can a woman go in love?

Chapter Two

However cosmic Godard's vision of prostitution, it is not the only social theme to be found in his films: there are others, more directly political. But even there we will see the same characteristic interaction between personal and social elements, and the same strength which proceeds, I think, from the tension between the two.

Godard's relation to politics and political themes has always been much more complex, more ambiguous, than that of the other directors of the New Wave—or at least of what is generally known as the *Cahiers* group. Like Truffaut, Godard went on record saying that he could only make films about things and people he knew. "It is not for me," he said, "to make a film about the dockers' strike at Nantes because I don't really know anything about it and I'd do it badly." On the other hand, as early as 1950, in an article called "For a Political Cinema" he wound up the essay by exhorting French scriptwriters looking for subjects to seek them in a study of the assessment of taxes, in the death of Philippe Henriot, or in the marvellous life of Danielle Casanova, Resistance martyr.

When he actually came to make films, however, he reverted to what we might call the Truffaut position, largely because, as he admitted, he knew so little of life that he could only copy it from the films he had seen. *A Bout de Souffle* was modelled much more on *Scarface* and other American thrillers than on any direct knowledge Godard had of the underworld milieu. The fact that, as he says, it didn't come out like *Scarface*, probably led him to reflect

A Bout de Souffle: Belmondo and victim

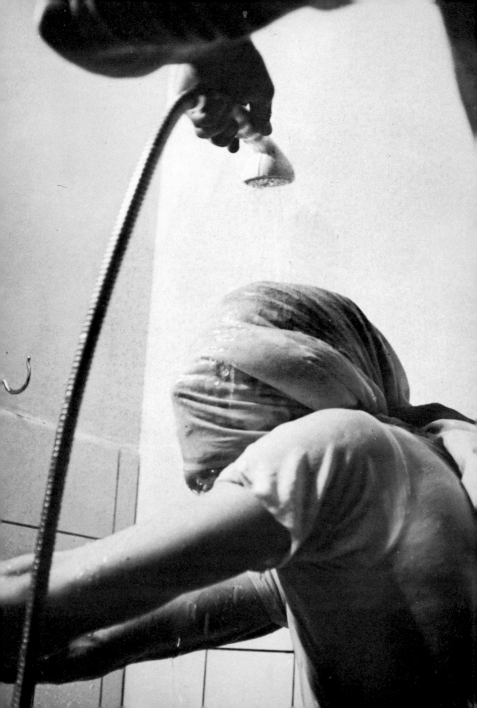

Le Petit Soldat: Michel Subor. The banality of evil

further on the problem, and the result was his second film, *Le Petit Soldat.*

While he was shooting the film, he resolutely maintained that the political aspects were simply the *données* of the scenario, that the action was not seen from a political point of view at all. But, of course, it very much was. On the other hand, Godard is above all thoroughly honest, and so a film by him about the repercussions of the Algerian situation could only be somewhat confused, because he himself was confused as to the rights and wrongs involved. "I wanted to show a confused mind in a confused situation," he said afterwards. "Well, that could be considered wrong, because perhaps one should not have been confused. But that's how it was. My film, in any case, was a kind of auto-critique."

This attitude is perhaps too defensive for, after all, at the time the film was made, the French were just about as undecided. According to public opinion polls at the time, as much as eighty per cent of the population didn't know what to think about the question, and, in fact, didn't want to think about it at all.

Le Petit Soldat was a film about a man with no ideals, who wanted desperately to find some. Like Jimmy Porter, he looked back nostalgically to the Spanish Civil War, when the lines were, or seemed to be, clearly drawn. In Godard's case his hero looked back also to 1944 when the French had an ideal, when they really seemed to believe in something.

Asking questions, says the hero of the film, is more important than finding answers, and *Le Petit Soldat* asked a lot of questions. The controversial torture scenes, which probably contributed as much as anything to getting the film banned for three years, were an attempt, not "to make the audience faint" but to make them think. The real horror was not so much in the actual torture as in the fact that the torturers did not find it particularly horrible—hence the frighteningly ordinary scenes in which the torture is interrupted by a girl delivering the weekly bundle of clean shirts. Or notice, too, the jar of hair-cream in the bathroom in which the torture takes place—another reminder of the banality of it all.

Godard once wanted to make a film about the concentration camps, but one which would be seen from the side of the torturers, as it were. It would be concerned with their practical, everyday problems: how to incinerate twenty bodies for the price of ten—cutting down on gas, etc. We would see typists carefully making their inventories of hair, teeth, etc. What would have been unbearable about such scenes, said Godard, was not the horror of them, but on the contrary, their completely normal and everyday aspect.

Of course, Godard is right: such a film would be much more frightening than one seen from the point of view of the victims, and that is why he so much admired Munk's *Passenger*, which goes part of the way along these lines. But it was statements like this which made many people accuse Godard of callousness, of unfeeling neutrality. And yet to be clear-sighted is not to be callous: understatement can often be more effective than pulling out all the stops; and perhaps the most frightening aspect of evil is its banality. In any case, whatever the Leftist objections at the time, *Le Petit Soldat* is now recognised even by them as being a faithful and powerful evocation of the situation seven years ago.

Curiously enough, *Le Petit Soldat* can also be looked upon as another addition to Godard's films on prostitution. For although Bruno doesn't believe in the cause for which he has been fighting, he nevertheless refuses to give in under torture. "Can one force people to do things in spite of themselves?" asked Godard. Which of course does 'reduce', if you like, *Le Petit Soldat* to a drama as much on a personal as on a political level. Nevertheless, it was an important step in Godard's career, although one might imagine that it took on even greater importance in his mind when it was banned. Perhaps the very idea that the film was so upsetting to the authorities gave him a new notion both of its power, and of their vulnerability.

The next two films were apolitical, but in his fifth, *Les Cara-biniers*, he boldly attacked one of the biggest subjects of our time, war. One can suggest all kinds of reasons for Godard's sudden change of direction. One could say that having brought his formal preoccupations to a successful, if temporary, conclusion with *Vivre sa Vie*, he was tempted to strike out on new ground.

Godard himself has declared that as he made more and more films and was forced to meet more and more kinds of people, from all levels of society, and to know them better, he began to be able to treat a wider range of characters and hence subject-matter than in his earlier films. But there is another, and perhaps more urgent, explanation. Godard's first feature film was shot just after de Gaulle came to power in 1958. It is no secret that, whatever the virtues of the de Gaulle régime may have been, it has led progressively to a greater indifference among the French to political questions, to what has been called the *dépolitisation* of France. This is perhaps also imputable to the average Frenchman's desire for a rest after the death-throes of the Fourth Republic; but many have felt this increasing political indifference to be a dangerous sign, and one which might well be a forerunner of Fascism. In any case, it is undeniable that Godard's films have become more politically oriented in inverse proportion to the degree of political awareness among his compatriots.

The first subject he tackled, then, was a simple one, one about which there could be little disagreement: a film against war. But it was unlike any other anti-war film that has ever been made. "I should have put on the credit titles," said Godard afterwards, "that

Les Carabiniers

it was a Fable. But an objective fable: I tried to film war objectively, without passion; with neither fear nor heroism, courage nor cowardice. As Franju filmed the abattoirs in *Le Sang des Bêtes*, but even without his close-ups, because a close-up is automatically emotional in its effect."

Most war films, however pacifist in intention, cannot avoid scenes which some viewers can take either as glorifications of the warlike spirit or as just plain exciting. Not with *Les Carabiniers*, which successfully re-creates the boredom, the futility, the absolute stupidity of war. So successfully, in fact, that many critics declared it to be the most ridiculous and stultifying film they had ever seen. It was not a success commercially, precisely because Godard had so completely achieved what he set out to do. But perhaps also because, being a fable, it was too generalised, and its relevance escaped the ordinary viewer. If this was a mistake, it was one that Godard was never to repeat.

In *Une Femme Mariée*, *Alphaville*, *Pierrot le Fou*, *Masculin*

Les Carabiniers

Féminin, and his last two films, his targets were to become much more specific. ("*Alphaville* is a fable on a realistic ground," said Godard.) But they were also to be much more closely related to his personal themes: he was to speak of *Pierrot le Fou* as a personal film but one connected with the violence and loneliness that lie so close to happiness. It sounds almost like E. M. Forster's "Only connect", but that is, in fact, characteristic of the later Godard. "Do you think you're a moralist?" the novelist Le Clézio asked him. The characteristic answer was, "Yes, oh yes. I think we all are. But one doesn't say it because it sounds pretentious." Tracking him even closer, two left-wing journalists said: "You talk about humanism; do you think you're a humanist?" To which Godard gave the only reply an honest, and a timid man could give. "Er, why yes, but . . . it's a pretty big word. But . . . yes, yes."

And of course he is. A preoccupation with formal values or personal themes need not stop a man from being either a humanist or a moralist, or prevent him from tackling political themes. As

43

the novelist Jorge Semprun put it, "Experimentation can only be formal. Content is not a subject for experiment, it is imposed on us, either by the world, by our ideas, or by our personal obsessions." As Godard himself said to Le Clézio, "We novelists and film-makers are condemned to an analysis of the world, of the real; painters and musicians aren't."

Godard's last three films, *Masculin Féminin*, *Made in U.S.A.*, and *Deux ou Trois Choses que je sais d'elle*, form a kind of trilogy of contemporary life, one which grew out of the earlier analysis of the consumer society in *Une Femme Mariée*, the North African situation in *Le Petit Soldat*, war in *Les Carabiniers*, robot society in *Alphaville*, and violence in *Pierrot le Fou*. But before considering this trilogy, several other matters must first be discussed. "An accusation of man's social condition," wrote Malraux, "can lead to the destruction of the system on which it is based." "And," he added, "the accusation of the human condition, in art, can lead to the destruction of the forms which accept it." And, *grosso modo*, as Godard would say, this hermetic statement is the subject of the next two chapters.

Chapter Three

"The distinguishing feature of modern art," wrote André Malraux, "is that it never tells a story. . . . Before the art of our time could come into its own, the art of dramatic fiction had to pass away, and it died hard." Indeed it did, for the reproach most often slung at Godard is that he can't tell a story; that there is never enough plot, and that what there is, is dramatically incoherent at best, arbitrary at worst. These objections are very real ones, and the admirer of Godard had best plead guilty on all counts, but reserve defence.

Godard does *not* 'tell stories'. Even his detractors, however, have to admit that he could if he wanted to, since most of them except *A Bout de Souffle* from their strictures. What they fail to recognise is that he doesn't *want* to. I am afraid this clamour for plot is related to the sad fact that films are still relegated to an inferior position in the arts, for the same people will accept a novel which doesn't have much plot. And, indeed, the contemporary novel is more and more orientated towards a 'dissolving of plot', to use Umberto Eco's phrase; whatever happens to Leopold Bloom or Mrs. Dalloway, or to Robbe-Grillet's nameless characters or Beckett's unnamable ones, is generally insignificant or inessential. Life, as Eco points out, is more like *Ulysses* than *The Three Musketeers*, but each of us is tempted to think more on the lines of *The Three Musketeers* than on those of *Ulysses* because we can generally only recall or judge past events by re-thinking them along the lines of the well-made novel. Therefore, it is perhaps not only that Godard's detractors refuse to allow the cinema the same freedom they allow the novel; perhaps they also obscurely feel that the cinema, being closer to life than the novel, *ought* to be more like they *imagine* life is, given that they imagine it more easily on *Three Musketeers* lines.

But for Godard the cinema is not just story-telling; in fact it is not even story-telling at all. "I consider myself an essay-writer," he said. "I write essays in the form of novels, or novels in the form of essays. I'm still as much of a critic as I ever was during the time of *Cahiers du Cinéma*. The only difference is that instead of writing criticism, I now film it."

This may be a new development for the cinema, but it is one that has existed in the other arts for nearly a hundred years. As even a committed critic like Sartre admits: "Since Mallarmé we have entered into a period in which art criticises itself. 'La Poésie Critique': thus Mallarmé defined his poetic epoch. Since then most art and literature criticises itself. For example, a sculptor—let's say Giacometti—tries to make a certain statue, not according to the usual recipes and principles, but by calling into question sculpture itself in the very statue he makes." This view was echoed by Godard—strangely enough in a review of Renoir's *Eléna et les Hommes*. "This film is art and at the same time a theory of art; beauty and at the same time the secret of beauty; cinema and at the same time an explanation of the cinema." He even went so far elsewhere as to say that "the whole New Wave can be defined, in part, by its new relationship to fiction and reality. . . ."

And Godard's films are a criticism of the cinema, a theory of the cinema; they are also essays and, above all, diaries. Like the story by Borgès that he quoted in an interview: "There once was a man who wanted to create a world; so he began by creating houses, provinces, valleys, rivers, tools, fish, lovers, etc., and at the end of his life, he noticed that this patiently elaborated labyrinth of forms was nothing other than his own portrait." So with Godard, who paints his own portrait in every film. To finish Malraux's phrase: "The anecdotal subject was bound to give way to the presence of the artist upon his own canvas."

But the cinema is a temporal art: unlike painting and sculpture, it can never be totally abstract because if one has to watch something for 90 minutes, one needs some support, some structure on which the film can be hung. Norman McLaren is fine in his way, but the idea of a feature-length McLaren fills at least one viewer with fear and trembling. (At this point I can hear the *avant-garde* all over Greenwich Village rising in fury to protest that since one can listen to an 'abstract' symphony for an hour, why not a film. No reason, I suppose, except that the eyes are either more demanding or less sensitive than the ears.) In any case, Godard *does* feel the need of a support. Either he begins with a news item or some real event in which he "can already see the profile of a legend" (as he wrote about Nick Ray's *True Story of Jesse James*) or he begins with a story. "I don't really like telling a story," he admits. "I prefer to use a kind of tapestry, a background on which I can embroider my own ideas. But I generally do need a story. A conventional one serves as well, perhaps even best." And one could say that the relationship of the original story to the finished film is that of the little waltz tune written by Diabelli to the monumental set of variations on it composed by Beethoven. But the best way to understand Godard's conception of the cinema is to look at the novels he has used as starting-points for his films. In so doing, one can see something of his creative process at work.

The first thing one notices is that his adaptations are generally based on inferior material. Unlike, say, Resnais, he prefers it that way: "Moravia's novel [*A Ghost at Noon*] is a nice novel for a train journey, full of classical old-fashioned sentiments. But it is with this kind of novel that one can make the best films." True enough; one has only to think of Welles and Booth Tarkington's *The Magnificent Ambersons*. This is not to say that Godard actually prefers, as literature, Dolores Hitchens (source of *Bande à Part*), or Lionel White (source of *Pierrot le Fou*); one of his favourite novels is *The Wild Palms*, but he doesn't want to make a film out of it. Rather, he said he would like to have his last two films shown, first a reel of *Made in U.S.A.*, then a reel of *Deux ou Trois Choses que je sais d'elle*, then a reel of *Made in U.S.A.*, etc., just as

Bande à Part: Sami Frey, Claude Brasseur, Danièle Girard,
Anna Karina

Faulkner mixed two stories in *The Wild Palms. That* would be his
adaptation of the novel.

The 'cheap' American thriller, translated into French and published in the popular *Série Noire*, has been a great source of
material for film directors. Usually, the novels are transplanted by
the film-makers into French locales, partly by preference, partly,
one supposes, for economy. However, there is generally something
left of the American atmosphere. For example, when Truffaut
filmed the late David Goodis's novel *Down There* in *Tirez sur le
Pianiste*, I think that even if one had not known the American

origin of the book, one might have felt it from the film. Since Truffaut followed the novel so closely, and in fact succeeded so completely in rendering its atmosphere, one could not but feel that the original material was non-indigenous. On the other hand, I am sure that few people who saw *Bande à Part* ever realised that it was based on a novel set in Los Angeles and called *Fool's Gold*. For one thing, the film is strongly rooted in Paris as a place: the Louvre, the Métro, the Place de la Nation, the suburbs. Secondly, the two boys themselves were made to seem even more typically French precisely by their fascination with imitating American gangsters as they had presumably read about them in the *Série Noire* or seen them in American films. In other words, nourished by the same material as Godard himself, they became all the more French.

The basic plot of the book is very close to that of *Bande à Part*—the two boys, Skip more delinquent than Eddie, the girl, Karen, who lives with her adopted aunt in whose house someone has stashed away a pile of money. Karen lets slip this information, and the boys plan a robbery. The first major difference between book and film is that Godard has left aside the rather cheap psychology that books of this kind are always at pains to trot out, hoping thus to give the basic story a fancy veneer. For example, there is a moment in the book when Karen's aunt discovers both that her mysterious lodger's things have been tampered with and that the amount of money is far greater than she has imagined. Slightly stunned, she meets Karen on the stairs:

"For a moment Mrs. Havermann paused. Her emotions had been stirred as they had not been in years. She was on the verge of panic, and the need to talk to someone was almost overpowering. Like an electric spark there seemed to flow between them a blaze of sympathy and compassion. There was in both a terrible need to communicate. . . . And for the first time in Mrs. Havermann's life, she felt the girl there as a living human being on whom she could depend, whose love she had earned and deserved. . . . But the words wouldn't come. In years of repression, of rejection, the loving and confiding words had withered and died. . . . In the next moment she would have spilled her panic and confusion, and Karen would have confessed all of Skip's plans. . . . Now there was only awkward silence."

None of this is in the film, and for two reasons, I think. First of all, this kind of 'psychology' would not appeal to Godard, and secondly, from the point of view of the plot and the basic idea of the film, nothing must stand in the way of the working out of the mechanism. Perhaps precisely because Godard is not interested in plot, he allows nothing to spoil its basic purity and inevitability of structure. Nothing, except his own kind of alienation techniques, like the English lesson in which the class is asked to translate back into English a passage from *Romeo and Juliet* in French; their knowledge of English will be graded on how close they come to Shakespeare's original words! This, or the lightning tour of the Louvre, Godard allows to break up the basic plot, perhaps because it really does break it up, while psychological meandering would only be a weakening decoration of it.

A good half of the book is devoted to the story of Skip's uncle, now quietly retired from a life of crime, and his attempts to come back by making a killing on the information Skip has given him. The Syndicate also wants to move in, and many chapters are devoted to this as well as to the connections between the Syndicate and the man from Las Vegas whose money both the boys and the Syndicate are planning to steal. In the film this whole subplot is reduced to no more than two or three tiny scenes: one in which the uncle discovers the plans for the robbery, and another in which he tries to steal the money, and he and his nephew are killed.

No thriller-writer would have been content with the bare bones of this two-boys-and-a-girl plot; but that was precisely what interested Godard, and that is what he took. So the whole epilogue of the book is cut: the escape of Karen and Eddie, on the run from the police up and down the California coast. One can't imagine, either, Godard filming Karen's remorse: "'I tried to hitch a ride on the highway. And then I saw,' her voice sharpened—'I saw what my whole life would be from then on. Just running. . . . We can take what's coming to us. Perhaps it won't be too bad. Perhaps a long time from now, we can see each other again. . . .'"

Apart from the revoltingly phoney moral tone, apart from the reliance on cliché, Godard had to give the film a happy end. Karen and Eddie (Odile and Franz in the film) sail off to the South Seas because this 'happy end' paradoxically only makes the film more hopelessly tragic. If it had ended with both going to jail, or even being killed, the audience would accept that as pure convention. By letting them get off scot-free, he almost forces the viewer to a critical reflection on the absurdity of the ending, and hence to conclude that it really couldn't have ended like that. Therefore, in his own mind, the viewer supplies the necessary tragic conclusion, and all the more forcefully because it has not been imposed upon him—he has supplied it himself.* I don't know for sure if this was Godard's intention, but, if it was, it would fit in with his otherwise slightly hermetic statement: "The cinema can be physically defined as a double movement which projects us towards others at the same time that it takes us back to the depths of ourselves: inside out is only right side out."

In any case, *Bande à Part* would seem to be constructed throughout on a kind of doubles principle: France-America; audience-director; novel-essay; documentary-fiction. "The Americans," says Godard, "know how to tell stories very well; the French, not at all. Flaubert and Proust don't know how to narrate; they do something else." This may or may not be true, but it is certainly true of Godard that he is always doing something else. For instance, the whole film could be seen as a kind of expanded metaphor of those sad inhabitants of the *banlieue* whose only escape from the boredom and ugliness of their daily lives is precisely in the cinema and the cheap American thriller which takes them out of themselves. And here Godard puts them right back in it, as it were. "In any case," he has said, "life and the unreal are inseparable. If you begin with life, you find unreality behind, and vice versa." Or, put even better, "the imaginary and the real are firmly separated and yet are both

---

* This may also be true of the 'happy end' of *Alphaville*.

one, like the Moebius curve which has at the same time both two sides and one side". Dolores Hitchens's basic plot provided the material for a documentary on the *vie de banlieue*. "You can either start with fiction," he said, "or with documentary. But whichever you start with, you will inevitably find the other." So *Bande à Part* is a 'Western de banlieue', and at the same time, another of Godard's portraits of the outsider in urban society. For no matter what material he starts out with—articles in *L'Express*, a novel by Lionel White, or a Maupassant short story (*Masculin Féminin*), it all comes out the same, so strong is his own personality and his own world.

If any further proof were needed, one has only to look at the Lionel White novel, *Obsession*, on which *Pierrot le Fou* was based. Slightly higher in literary merit than the Dolores Hitchens, it tells a kind of Lolita story fairly well. Conrad, the hero, is an out-of-work advertising executive(!) who falls very hard for a seventeen-year-old baby-sitter. After driving her home at the end of a drunken party, he spends the night only to wake up to find a third person in her flat: a corpse. She killed him, she says, to keep him from slicing up Conrad. They take it on the lam, since no one, apparently, would believe the self-defence story, and the rest of the book is a long ramble round America, with Conrad slowly realising how deeply he has got himself into a criminal world and how difficult he is going to find it to get out. His sexual obsession with the girl keeps him going until he finally realises just how evil she is, how ready to doublecross him. He strangles her, calls the police, and the novel ends with the girl,

"Allie, where I left her, naked on the bed in the next room. But I am no longer thinking of Allie. I am thinking once again of my wife Marta and of my two children. I hope they will understand this last thing and know that it was the only thing I could do, that it was the only way I could cure myself of an obsession which I can't hope to explain. For some reason I have no fear and no regrets. For the first time in more years than I can remember, I am at peace with myself."

Pierrot le Fou: Karina and Belmondo →

The novel, as a property, seems to have floated round Paris for a few years. It was eventually proposed to Godard with Sylvie Vartan in the Lolita role. He turned this down: he didn't want a young girl, partly because Kubrick's *Lolita* was coming out, and partly because he didn't like the old man/young girl element which rendered the whole story more pathetic than tragic. Then it was going to be filmed with Anna Karina and Richard Burton, but Godard turned down Burton as being too *Hollywoodisé*. Finally, the casting was set with Belmondo and Karina.

Godard didn't want to make *Lolita* all over again; but neither did he want to redo *La Chienne* (although there is a reference to the Renoir film in *Pierrot le Fou*). The partners had to be more equal. "I wanted," he said, "to do a kind of *You Only Live Once*, a story of the last romantic couple left alive, the descendants of *La Nouvelle Héloïse* and *Werther*." It didn't quite turn out like that.

It didn't turn out like that because, for one thing, Godard doesn't write scripts. "I just write out the strong moments of the film," he says, "and that gives me a kind of *trame* of seven or eight points." "*Pierrot le Fou* isn't really a film, it's an attempt at cinema [*une tentative de cinéma*]. Life is the subject, with 'Scope and colour as its attributes. . . . Life on its own as I would like to capture it, using pan shots on nature, *plans fixes* on death, brief shots, long takes, soft and loud sounds, the movements of Anna or Jean-Paul. In short, life filling the screen as a tap fills a bathtub that is simultaneously emptying at the same rate. The whole ending was invented on the spot, unlike the beginning which was organised. It's a sort of Happening, but one that was controlled and dominated. Two days before I began I had nothing, absolutely nothing. Oh well, I did have the book. And a certain number of locations. What helps to give me ideas are locations. . . . I've got a notion that when Bresson or Demy shoot a film they have an idea of the world that they are trying to put on to the screen; or, which comes to the same thing, an idea of the cinema they are trying to apply to the world. For them, cinema and the world are moulds to be filled, while in *Pierrot* there is neither mould nor matter."

"Oh well, I did have the book."—Yes, but in this particular

case, I think the 'support' was not strong enough for all that Godard wanted—or began to want in the process of making the film—to put into it. As in the book, and as in half of Godard's films, the man represents the contemplative principle, the woman the active. That is putting it at its noblest: Marianne knows exactly what she wants, and Ferdinand knows only that he wants her, and having her, to lead a quiet life, reading and meditating on his island paradise. But Marianne isn't content with this: she's bored. There's nothing on his island but "birth, copulation and death". So when Godard says that the violence of our time had to appear in *Pierrot le Fou* because it threatens the happiness of us all, one says, yes, of course, but this couple could never be happy, whether or not her brother were a gun-runner, or whether he actually is her brother or not. The murders committed in the film, the blood spilled, eventually do separate the couple, but how long would they have lasted in any case?

Furthermore, there is something wrong in the dosage of plot and essay—either there is too much plot or not enough, because in spite of its beautiful moments *Pierrot le Fou* does not seem to me to hold together as well as some of Godard's other films. If the basic *trame* were either stronger or weaker, then interruptions like Raymond Devos's little music-hall turn, the Bassiak song, and the Vietnam playlet would not have such destructive force. As we will see in Godard's last three films, *Masculin Féminin*, *Made in U.S.A.*, and *Deux ou Trois Choses que je sais d'elle*, a strong grounding in reality serves him best as a springboard for his essays or diaries.

Meanwhile, we can note that current political issues crop up in *Pierrot le Fou* more than in any of the preceding films. Even as Ferdinand drives Marianne home in the second reel of the film, the car radio broadcasts the latest news from Vietnam; the aftermath of the Algerian situation makes an early appearance; as does the war in the Yemen, Angola, even the Kennedy assassination: Marianne's rifle is the same make as the one (or should one say—one of the ones) used in Dallas. But these jottings on contemporary violence are not sufficiently integrated, much as Godard's avowed attempt to make this a film "about the spaces between people" is

59

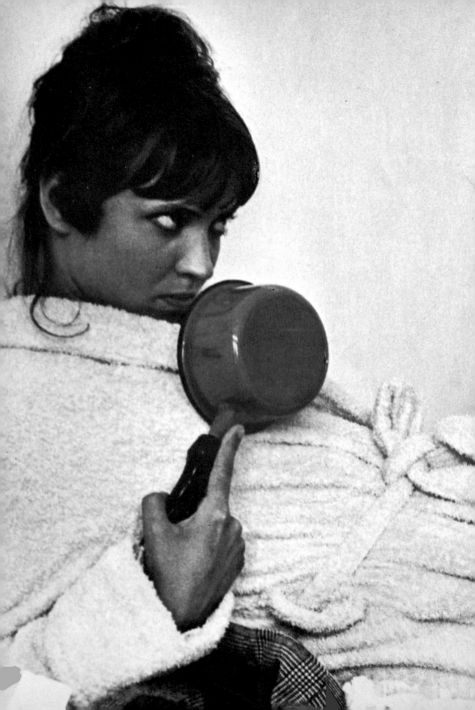

Pierrot le Fou: Karina, Belmondo, and "Vision of Horror in San Domingo"

undercut by the interest he willy-nilly generates in the plot itself. "I've found an idea for a novel," says Ferdinand/Pierrot. "Not to write the life of a man, but only life, life itself. What there is between people, space . . . sound and colours. . . . There must be a way of achieving that; Joyce tried, but one must, must, be able . . . to do better." And so Godard will—in *Deux ou Trois Choses que je sais d'elle.*

A Ghost at Noon, the Moravia novel on which *Le Mépris* is based, is something of a special case. In spite of what he says about it being a railway journey novel, it *is* a cut above that; and in some ways, Godard—either through choice, or because of the insistence of his producer, Carlo Ponti—stuck rather closer to it than he did to the American novels, with two exceptions. First of all, the novel is told in the first person, and if we believe the narrator, which I assume we must, then we must believe his version of the incident which sets off the action. In the film, we are never sure whether

Paul is lying when he says that he was delayed fifteen minutes by a silly accident in getting to the producer's house. In fact, it looks as though he is lying, and therefore Camille's belief that he has come late on purpose so that the producer might have time to make a pass at her seems valid. In the novel, the narrator tells us that this is not true. It doesn't make too much difference in the end, but it is an example of Godard's greater subtlety, and also an example of his belief that this relationship, like all the others in his films, is doomed from the start because of the fundamental—almost metaphysical—impossibility of any such relationship lasting.

Furthermore, Godard leaves out an incident in which the narrator remembers his wife catching him with lipstick on his shirt, thus removing another 'psychological' justification for her falling out of love.

But these are minor matters, perhaps. Much more important is the way in which Godard has introduced into the film—or actually made *of* the film—a documentary on film-making in Italy. First of all, the director of *The Odyssey*, who is described by Moravia as being a fairly well-known German, no Lang, of course, is transformed by Godard into precisely . . . Fritz Lang. (I seem to remember there was talk at some point after the war of Pabst making *The Odyssey* in Italy, so perhaps Godard has drawn upon that, too.) In the book, with the exception of the German, all the characters are Italians. This Godard changes: Paul and Camille are French; Prokosch, the producer, is an American; and he introduces an entirely new and very important character—that of Francesca, the Italian quadrilingual interpreter, played by Giorgia Moll. Everyone, naturally, speaks his own language, and so Francesca plays a significant part (as she would do in real life) as translator/interpreter. Her continuous translation adds a very important motif to the film, and in a sense she points up the difficulties the characters have in communicating with each other on a profound level by helping them to communicate on a basic language level.* The film world in the novel is only a vague back-

---

* All this was cut in the Italian version, in which, incredibly, everyone speaks Italian, and Miss Moll's dialogue had to be invented out of nothing to cover up.

Le Mépris: Brigitte Bardot, Fritz Lang, Michel Piccoli,
Jack Palance

ground: in *Le Mépris* it takes on much more importance, as it naturally would, given Godard's interest in documentary. Furthermore, perhaps because he is not a Roman like Moravia, much more attention is paid to the Italianate aspects of the situation. Not just in the colour, but in the peeling walls of a run-down Cinecittà, the little variety theatre where they all go to look over an actress, the screening-room with Lumière's famous line "The cinema is an invention without any future" emblazoned on the masking.

Throughout the film—sometimes aided by Moravia, but mostly not—we find a constant interchange between the story of Paul and Camille and the handicaps of the 'international' film, the co-production, as well as the basic problems of film-making itself: the script conferences, the battles with the incredibly stupid producer (Jack Palance has a field-day here with his little book of inane proverbs). Given Godard's great admiration for Lang, one supposes that his own appearance in the film as Lang's assistant is meant as a kind of *hommage*; on the other hand, it is typically paradoxical, for it is Godard who is directing Lang.

Structurally, Godard has made a very important change from the book: he has condensed all the many husband-and-wife scenes from the first half of the novel into a major sequence in their flat which lasts no less than *30 minutes*, almost a third of the film. This is extremely significant because it points up a development in Godard's films away from conventional narrative techniques towards a kind of block-like tableau construction. As he has broken down conventional narrative into simple narrative elements, which themselves are broken up with quasi-documentary sequences, at the same time the actual construction of his films has changed: from the jump-cut, one could say, to the conversation sequence.

When *A Bout de Souffle* first came out, everyone was either shocked or excited by the 'rapid' style of cutting employed by Godard. As he said at the time, "I discovered in *A Bout de Souffle* that when a discussion between two people became boring and tedious, one could just as well cut between the speeches. I tried it once, and it went very well, so I did the same thing right through the film." The jump-cuts certainly speeded up the film, eliminating all unnecessary transitions and matching shots. He did away with dissolves, too (*A Bout de Souffle* has only one), partly for speed, and partly because, "I prefer simply putting things side by side." Furthermore, as Godard remarked apropos of a Tashlin film, "the *découpage* of comic strips is aesthetically years ahead of film *découpage*. Within each strip, the change of shot is done with an inventive boldness that is missing now from the French cinema." Well, he put it back, but it is interesting that when one looks at *A Bout de Souffle* now, the famous jump-cuts seem to have disappeared; one hardly notices them, so permanent and ubiquitous a feature of contemporary film style have they become. The same holds true, by the way, for the hand-held camera shots which caused such a furore at the time: they, too, are almost invisible.

What one does notice, on the other hand, is that even in his first film, Godard had begun his form of block construction: the big bedroom scene between Belmondo and Seberg is already quite long. In *Le Petit Soldat* there will be two similar sequences, one in which Bruno photographs Véronica (to the sound of Haydn), and the other a long conversation scene towards the end. This paradoxical alternation of brief shots and longish sequences—themselves made up of many brief shots, but somehow soldered together —reaches its height in *Vivre sa Vie*, *Les Carabiniers*, and *Le Mépris*.

To be sure, the big apartment sequence in *Une Femme est une Femme* already lasted over 15 minutes; and there is a very long fixed shot later in the café when the story which was eventually to form the plot of Godard's episode in *Paris vu par . . .* is told—in fact the whole café sequence lasts 13 minutes, what with the telling of the story and the juke box record of an Aznavour song, "Tu t' laisses aller". But in *Vivre sa Vie*, broken as it is into twelve 'tableaux', the process is formalised. "I built *Vivre sa Vie* in tableaux," said Godard, "to accentuate the theatrical side of the film. Besides, this division corresponded to the external view of things which best allowed me to give the feeling of what was going on *inside*. In other words, a contrary procedure to that used by Bresson in *Pickpocket*, in which the drama is seen from within. How can one render the 'inside'? I think, by staying prudently outside."

Vivre sa vie: Peter Kassowitz and Karina. The mating dance

But it is quite clear that there are other, more formal reasons for this construction in *Vivre sa Vie*, most of which we will come to in the next chapter. Meanwhile, I think we can say that as progressively plot is more and more left behind in favour of something else, so the style of Godard's films had to evolve towards the sequence system. The first long sequence in the film is the one in the bar, with Nana and Paul; it lasts almost 7 minutes, and most of the time we see the characters' backs. The long scene in which Nana writes her letter lasts over 8 minutes; while the great 'mating dance' in the billiard-room lasts only 3 minutes, and is made up of practically only four very prolonged shots following Nana round the billiard-table. There is one cut to the walls as the shot becomes subjective, then we go back to Nana, and finally cut to Nana at rest against a column. The point I am trying to make here is not so much the length of the shots (not, after all, so very unusual) but the alternation of these fairly long shots with two flash-shots, one of the juke box, one of the young man she is trying to seduce—which is why I said 'practically' only four shots.

The tableaux themselves vary in length from 2 minutes to $10\frac{1}{2}$ minutes, some of them containing long sequences like the ones I mentioned, others made up of many very brief shots. Furthermore, there is simultaneously another time scheme in the film, that of the soundtrack; this is treated in a very unrealistic manner, and will be discussed in the next chapter.

Les Carabiniers further developed this block construction: the 10-minute sequence in which the women persuade Michel-Ange and Ulysse to enlist, but most extraordinary of all, the famous 12-minute postcard sequence, which is almost entirely devoted to the displaying of the postcard/trophies the men have brought back from the war. But it is with *Le Mépris* that Godard goes the limit in the aforementioned 30-minute sequence in Paul and Camille's flat, a sequence which, as I said, resumes whole chapters of the novel.

The dramatic advantages of such a sequence are clear: it helps to express the Classic unity, the serenity which Godard felt suited *The Odyssey*: after all, it is not for nothing that he gives to Lang in the film the Classical ideas that the producer holds in the novel, while conversely, the silly Freudian approach of Rheingold, the director in the novel, is given to the producer in the film.

"The principle of this sequence," predicted Godard, "will be the same as that of the hotel room in *A Bout de Souffle*. But that scene was linear from beginning to end; it began, continued, and ended in the same tone; this one has to be composed in such a way that it rises to a paroxysm, calms down, rises up again to an emotional height, sinks down again, and then rises for a third time. The first culminating moment will be the abortive love scene; the second Camille's false departure, and the third Paul's access of rage." It didn't work out quite so mathematically. The sequence is complicated with a flash-forward to Capri and a flash-backward to the studios. In any case, although one may think Godard's sequences work to some kind of mathematical formula, they don't; or at least not to any mathematics yet invented. For him, montage is not done with a stop-watch, it's rather a question of heart-beats; and they, of course, vary constantly and subtly. For example, this sequence was supposed to last only 20 minutes; and yet it goes on for half an hour.

But the interesting point is that as Godard developed this technique of longer and longer sequences, he at the same time began to play around with the possibilities of *montage court*. As early as 1956 he thought of the possibility that a camera movement cut in four could be more effective than the shot kept as filmed. This was precisely what he was to do in *Vivre sa Vie*, in the tracking shot in a café scene which is cut into by the sound of machine-gun fire, and correspondingly broken into pieces.

This was to be his line after *Le Mépris*. Having achieved the ultimate, perhaps, in a sequence which lasted nearly a third of the film, he was largely to abandon this technique. In the later films we will find a progression towards a greater fragmentation of the image. The shock cuts and brief shots were used in *A Bout de Souffle* for economy of means, to get the film moving faster. In the films after *Le Mépris* (but, given Godard's dialectical pulls, long before, too), he uses this fragmentation to make us perceive certain dramatic and visual relationships, to mystify—in the sense of fully rendering those basic ambiguities of life of which he is always so conscious—but most of all, I think, for almost abstract, visual reasons. In *Une Femme Mariée, Masculin Féminin,* and *Deux ou Trois Choses que je sais d'elle*, where he is not relying nearly so much on story but rather on a certain kind of sociological document, this abstract treatment of shot and montage will provide a form for the otherwise shapeless documentary material. Even in *Pierrot le Fou* and *Alphaville*, both of which have fairly developed plot-lines, we will notice the same phenomenon at work. And it is precisely in this relationship between subject and form that Godard reveals himself to be the most exciting film-maker of the 1960s.

Chapter Four

In an interview, Anna Karina made a curious comment on Demy's *Les Parapluies de Cherbourg*: "All their clothes come from Dior. And yet with dresses worth 500,000 francs on their backs, they cry woe and misery and sell their jewels. And you can smell their expensive perfume from 500 yards away. Of course, it doesn't matter in Demy's film, because it's meant to be a fairy-tale. But I don't see myself playing in one of my husband's films wearing a Chanel dress."

Curious, silly, and yet significant, for of all French directors Godard stands out by his insistence on, his belief in, the *real*. An anecdote from the continuity-girl on *Alphaville* brings this out pertinently: "The film was shot, you might say, without any extra light; in the dark, in fact. For one scene, Coutard said, 'I can add a bit of light and by closing the lens, it will come to the same thing —no one will notice the difference.' But Godard refused: it had to be real. So he shot without lights; he used very fast film, but even so. It became the joke of the film—'It's too dark to see anything. . . . So what, we're shooting just the same.' The result: several thousand feet of film were 'unusable'. But Godard didn't reshoot them entirely. Some of them were scrapped, but others went, just as they were, into the film. The most extraordinary thing of all is that they are some of the best things in the whole film."

Even on *Une Femme est une Femme*, his only film to be made in a studio, Godard worked as he would have done on location. Ceilings

were built solely to prevent the technicians from lighting the sets from above. The lighting-men were startled, to say the least, but this way Godard got the effect he was after—a greater naturalism.

This insistence on the real goes a long way back in Godard's mind: in a review of *Orfeu Negro* in 1959, he deplored Marcel Camus's "folly in believing he could *compete* with the sunlight of Rio de Janeiro with the help of coloured gelatine slides." Furthermore, he said, the film did not really capture the essence of Rio: walking down the Avenida Vargas, Camus just couldn't have heard the sambas coming out of the portable radios blaring from every shop.

Godard's use of colour points up this insistence on the real. True, it developed gradually. For *Une Femme est une Femme*, he says, "I had a décor and I chose my colours." For *Le Mépris*, he looked for locations; as for the colours, well, they came as they were. "I didn't paint a grey wall white because I preferred white; instead I looked for a white wall, whereas for *Une Femme est une Femme*, I would have painted the wall white. In *Une Femme est une Femme*, I tried to use colour dramatically. In *Le Mépris*, no. *Une Femme est une Femme* was the first time for me; with such a wonderful toy as colour, you play with it as much as you can. But in *Le Mépris*, the more natural, less fabricated, Italian colours corresponded perfectly to what I wanted, so I didn't do any painting or arranging."

"The big difference between the cinema and literature," as he told the novelist Jean-Marie Le Clézio, "is that in the cinema the sky is there. One never has to say, is the sky blue or grey? It's just *there*. . . . I never have the feeling I am differentiating between life and creation. On the other hand, for someone like Flaubert, it was a great problem whether to describe the sky or the sea as blue or grey or blue-grey. If the sky is blue, I film it blue."

This attitude applies to black and white, too, or at least it began to apply around the time of *Vivre sa Vie*. Before, says Godard, he was very careful about the colour of things, even in black and white. In *Vivre sa Vie*, however, what was black was black, and white, white. The actors all wore their usual clothes, the only

73

exception being Anna Karina: for her a skirt and sweater were bought.

Almost more important, however, is the application of Godard's documentary bias to sound. For even in the most so-called realist film, sound has always been an exception, ever since the early days of the talkies when ways were found to get round recording problems. All the Italian neo-realist films were dubbed, sometimes by the actual players, but as often as not by others. Naturalism of sound has always been cheerfully sacrificed to audibility. As Godard said, half-jokingly, if a man goes behind a wall, the audience doesn't expect to see him. But they still expect to hear him as clearly as if he were in front of the camera. All this was going to change in his films.

Again, not right away. The first two films were post-synchronised: *Une Femme est une Femme* was his first experience with direct sound and *Vivre sa Vie* brought this new technique to a head. Jean Collet, who followed the shooting of the film, reported in *La Revue du Son* the revolutionary news that the film was entirely shot with direct sound, both dialogue and noises. And, what's more, on a single tape. It was therefore, perhaps, the first 'commercial' film made outside a studio without any kind of sound montage. The mixing was restricted to the addition of the music. Most films, however realistically shot, are generally post-synchronised, the noises are always fabricated, and the sound-mixer finds himself with at least three or four tracks to blend together.

In some cases, of course, the mixing was done live on the spot, and several microphones were used; but in others, as in the first sequence in the café, only one microphone was used to capture both the dialogue and the atmospheric noises of the café. Generally when one hears a juke box in a film, a disc has been recorded directly on to tape, with a little bass added to imitate the low-fidelity boom. In this café scene, the juke box was actually recorded live. The same is true, we are told, for the juke box in the billiard-room sequence later in the film.

The continuity-girl on *Une Femme Mariée* recorded another example of this insistence on real sound: "Godard always wants to keep as much as possible of the actual shooting—if there are some unexpected noises off, they are retained. Unless, of course, the unexpected comes from the equipment and not from 'life': the noise of a camera, of a tracking shot. In *Une Femme Mariée* there was a long tracking shot at Orly Airport, and the noise of the camera squeaking over the rails came through. Everyone said, well, let it be, there are all kinds of strange noises at airports, no one will notice, they'll just think it's something else. But no, Godard insisted it must be reshot." In a film like *Les Carabiniers*, where lack of money prevented him from direct sound recording, he nevertheless held to his obsession with truth. Each rifle-shot, each explosion, was recorded separately, and then re-mixed, even though, as he admitted, they could have bought them all from Darryl Zanuck (who had just shot *The Longest Day*). Each aeroplane, each gun had its own real sound. No Heinkel sound for a shot of a Spitfire; no Beretta sound for a Thompson machine-gun.*

Why, one might ask, this tiresome, even pedantic insistence on the *real*? The answer, of course, is clear: Godard is interested in capturing time, the fleeting moment preserved like the proverbial fly in amber for all eternity. The moment is what makes the cinema beautiful, he says. It is for that it was invented, to record the instant. The reason he so liked the films of Ingmar Bergman was that Bergman is a film-maker of the moment. Each of his films is born, said Godard, in a reflection of the hero on a moment in time: a meditation which starts from a snapshot. "A twenty-fourth of a second which is metamorphosed and prolonged for an hour and a half. The world between two flickers of the eyelids, the sadness between two heart-beats, the joy of living between two hand-claps." The importance of the American comedy of the 1930s to

---

* Godard even once said that although he longed to make a film about ancient Rome, he would never be able to, because of course he would insist that the actors speak Latin. And more recently, he abandoned his project for filming *La Bande à Bonnot* because, set at the turn of the century, it would have to be done in costume and he personally didn't know how to design costumes. Even if he could, they wouldn't be real.

Pierrot le Fou: Karina and Belmondo at the beginning of the film's most extraordinary sequence, the series of shots indicating the various possibilities of their escaping from Paris. The first sequence ever shot in the conditional tense →

Godard was that it brought back rapidity of action, it allowed one to let oneself go to the full enjoyment of the passing moment. The 'grace' of *The Pajama Game* came from its quality of having been snapped—or shot—live, as it were. Life captured. And this in some respects explains the 'look' of many of Godard's films. He, too, wants to give the impression of snatching life, the impression of an amateur film. In a film like Preminger's *Fallen Angel*, Godard somewhat perversely even likes that scene in which the camera has to track so fast to keep Linda Darnell full in frame, that you can actually see the assistants pulling the extras out of the way of its path. He gets from it a real feeling of directness.

As an explanation of his obsession with capturing the passing moment, Godard once quoted Cocteau's lines about *Orphée*: "The cinema films death at work. The person you are filming is in the process of getting older, and one day will die. Therefore, you are filming a minute of death at work." Painting is immobile: "the cinema is interesting because it captures the mortal side of life." Like Goethe's Faust, Godard is continually bidding time to stop, to leave us with this moment of supreme beauty. Or sadness, or tragedy. "There is just a moment," said Godard, "when things cease to be a mere spectacle, a moment when a man is lost, and when he shows that he is lost."

Time is his enemy, as it is ours. In *Le Petit Soldat*, Bruno accepts a bet that he won't fall for Véronica. As a test, he asks her to shake her head, fluffing out her hair. She does, and struck by the beauty of this most passing of moments, he pays up: he has succumbed.

Godard's insistence on the real brings with it fringe benefits, too. For example, in the scene in which Nana first gives herself over to prostitution, the unexpected noise of a heavy truck outside the room rises in an appropriate dramatic crescendo. Or, as Collet tells us, in the very last sequence, at the moment of Nana's death, the bell of a near-by hospital suddenly began to ring in the silence of the deserted streets. Because of his belief in the moment, Godard can accept these magnificent opportunities which spring from the situation itself, these bonuses offered to art by life.

← *Pierrot le Fou*: Anna Karina

Of course, one of the essential characteristics of the filmed image is its eternal presence: as Robbe-Grillet said, in the cinema the verbs are always in the present tense. And yet, some paintings have also captured the eternal present. One thinks first of all of Vermeer, who was also, in a sense, a painter of reality, one whose subjects were drawn from the banality of everyday life. But often the beauty in both Vermeer and Godard comes from gestures or movement. The shot in almost every Godard film of a girl agitating her hair is not so different from Vermeer's capturing for all time a girl trying on a necklace in front of a mirror, or a servant pouring out milk into a jug: the necklace poised in mid-air, the milk caught passing from pitcher to bowl. (An incidental comparison would also show that both Vermeer and Godard always insist on *showing* their light source—the ever-present window in Vermeer is countered by the light which comes from windows in Godard, and hardly ever, as we have seen, from artificially placed lights.) Like Vermeer, Godard accepts the true light source—accepts and glories in it. Both seem to share an almost puritanical belief in the value of naked reality. Then, too, Vermeer has that Baroque sense of time which chooses the culminating moment, singled out and immortalised. Time is made to stop, the eternal flux is seized at an ideal moment and retained. Furthermore, Vermeer glories in ordinary subjects, ordinary objects. For both Godard and Vermeer, a window, a chair, can be—are made to be—seen as objects of extreme beauty.

However, neither Godard nor Vermeer is content simply to glorify everyday life: neither is a naturalistic scene painter. The most important thing about Godard's films for me is the way in which, like Vermeer, he transforms the everyday into an artistic creation through the power of abstraction. It has been said that Vermeer, like El Greco, immortalised a moment of time; and that, like Raphael, he took the painting *out* of time by freezing it in Classic perfection. In other words, a synthesis, a fusion of two great tendencies of art: Baroque and Classic, the one a triumph over time, the other over space. And the beauty in both Godard and Vermeer comes from precisely this fusion, from the

Vermeer's "Woman with Necklace". *Berlin Museum*

momentarily resolved contradiction between abstraction and reality, stasis and movement.

For Godard is as much interested in abstraction—both visual and aural—as he is in the mere seizing of the moment, as he is in narration, as he is in content. And it is the tensions created between the demands of reality and the demands of abstraction that have created his greatest films. Godard himself seems increasingly aware of this. In an interview of March 1967, he said: "I construct with the pieces that reality gives me. I like to think that I am a *workman.* I make an object which is 'me' and also 'independent of me'. Some of my effects crop up in the course of 'manufacturing' the object. But isn't this also true of the artisan? He has an idea of the whole,

A Bout de Souffle: Jean Seberg

but in details, he lets himself be guided by the grain of the wood. I also like to compare myself with a mathematician. When I was a *lycée* student, I wanted to study mathematics, or at least thought I wanted to. I liked the idea of pure research. What I've just said is not very coherent, is it: a workman who creates a physical object and a mathematician who is only concerned with pure ideas. But perhaps both are compatible, after all. The two things working together produce, almost involuntarily, some kind of mystical inspiration."

And in fact, he is right; the two ideas are not incompatible, or rather they can work together dialectically. And in this, Godard's films often resemble many of the most recent products of visual art,

Vivre sa Vie: the death of Nana

84

in which chance and accident have an important role (the 'grain of the wood' played a major part in Abstract Expressionist painting, and the combination of reality and abstraction in Pop Art play a larger part than many people realise).

I was once taken to task by Pauline Kael for writing about pure form in *La Notte*. At the risk of upsetting the lady again, I would like now to examine pure form in Godard—with the proviso that its purity is conditioned by its impure interaction with the other elements of his work.

As early as 1956, Godard had already proclaimed that basic idea which was to inform all his films from *Vivre sa Vie* onwards. "Montage will give back to the *pris sur le vif* all its ephemeral grace; it will metamorphose chance into fate." This was, then, a conscious choice on Godard's part. But a theoretician like Umberto Eco maintains that even when a television director is transmitting *live*, one can see the interaction between the passive opening of the several cameras to the thousand possibilities before them, and the 'plot': that is to say, the thread that the director proposes, by establishing—even in a split second—the relationship between the events he chooses to transmit. And Godard, who is so insistent, as we have seen, on absolute realism, can nevertheless decide, well in advance, that a certain sequence will last 10 minutes, another 30 seconds. He builds up a sketch of the rhythm of the film before he begins to shoot. But, much more important, *after* the shooting he will edit a scene so as to give it a meaning—sometimes a different one from what has been shot. "Sometimes," he says, "I have shots that were badly filmed, because I lacked time or money. Putting them together creates a different impression; I don't reject this; on the contrary, I try to do my best to bring out this new idea."

Some examples: *Vivre sa Vie* was the first film in which these principles were put into play in a systematic form. The credits of the film are superimposed on three shots of Anna Karina. First we see her left profile, then a full front view, and finally a right profile. But, as I said earlier, editing for Godard is not so much a matter of the stop-watch as of the heart-beat, so even in this classic triad, there are variations. Towards the end of the full front shot of Karina, she looks up, giving us a slightly different view. So much for the visual pattern. At the same time, the sound has also been patterned, almost but not quite to correspond to the visuals. The left profile shot is accompanied by music for its first 23 seconds; the next 25 seconds are accompanied by silence. At the 48th second of the credits we cut to the front view and the music begins again, continuing for only 24 seconds; the last 16 seconds of this second shot, including the 8 in which Karina looks up, are silent again. The right view of Karina begins with music again, which continues for 26 seconds, and the last 21 seconds of this shot are silent. In other words, the image falls into a three-shot pattern of 48 seconds/40 seconds/47 seconds, or almost equal thirds. But the sound-silence pattern breaks up into near-sixths: music—23 seconds; silence—25 seconds; music—24 seconds; silence—16 seconds; music—26 seconds; silence—21 seconds. This is the most rigidly formal example in the film, perhaps because Godard felt that the credits needed a stronger pattern than the action of the film itself.

A careful examination of the first sequence of *Vivre sa Vie* will give us a better idea of how Godard counterpoints reality with abstraction. You will remember that this was a scene recorded live on the spot in a real café, without any lights. In other words, news-reel style. The scene is composed of only four shots. The first, a back view of Nana seated at the bar, lasts 1 minute 46 seconds. During this shot, however, the camera pans a little to the right to pick up Paul's hands, but basically stays on Nana. The second shot lasts 3 minutes 3 seconds and is more varied: it begins on Paul's back, pans to Nana, returns to Paul, goes back to Nana, then closer in on Nana, and finally pans slowly right to Paul, who by now has turned sufficiently to the left so that we can at last see him properly. The third shot begins on Paul, but soon pulls back and follows him and Nana to the juke box. After 33 seconds, the fourth shot picks up Nana and Paul in front of the juke box; they listen and talk, the camera pans left, and the shot and the tableau end—this fourth shot has lasted 1 minute 17 seconds. To resume: four shots lasting respectively 106, 183, 33, and 77 seconds, making a total of 399 seconds in all.

As in the credits sequence, the music will follow a slightly different pattern. The first 1 minute 45 seconds of the sequence will be mute, almost, but not quite, tallying with the 1 minute 46 seconds of the first shot. Then the music begins, runs for 23 seconds, and stops short a few seconds before the first pan of the second shot. Silence resumes for the next 1 minute 41 seconds, and music begins only after the fourth pan of the second shot and will continue for 1 minute 33 seconds, stopping a $\frac{1}{2}$ second before the end of the third shot. Silence lasts a second or two, and then the natural sound of the juke box takes over for the rest of the tableau. To resume, the pattern runs as follows: silence—105 seconds; music—23 seconds; silence—101 seconds; music—93 seconds; silence—11 seconds; music—67 seconds.

Since Godard treats silence as he does music, that is to say, absence of music has the same importance as its presence for him—just as it does, by the way, in the works of Webern and other contemporary composers—we can tabulate the visual and aural duration of this sequence thus:

VISUAL	106	183	33	77		
AURAL	105	23	101	93	11	67

Thus we discover that, give and take a few seconds, and notwithstanding the division of the visuals into four sections and the sound/silence into six, the sequence as a whole divides fairly neatly into *three* sections. This is not an exact division, and is surely one of which the casual or even the not so casual viewer might be totally unaware. But this is not the point: Godard has presumably felt the need of imposing on this rawly shot raw material a high degree of form, and although the spectator is no more aware of it than is the casual concertgoer of how a fugue is composed, its effect is nevertheless felt.

Vivre sa Vie: Karina and Sady Rebbot in the 'pendulum' scene

In the same film there is an extraordinary sequence in which Nana applies for a job in a brothel: it begins with her carefully writing the letter; she is then joined by her future protector. A longish scene follows with the two of them seated at a café table. Rather ingenuously, Godard said that the pendulum-like movement of the camera in this scene corresponded to a 'technical' idea. "I didn't want to keep the same angle throughout the scene, and at the same time I didn't want to change the shot because I couldn't see any valid reason to do so; therefore, the only way was to move the camera." Perhaps. The resulting sequence, however, is extraordinary for the rigour with which he seems to have calculated the length of time the camera stays on any one object, the length of time it takes to move from right to left, left to right, or from right to centre, and then to left. It is, in fact, a carefully worked out choreography for the camera, but one that is almost certainly

Une Femme Mariée: still life

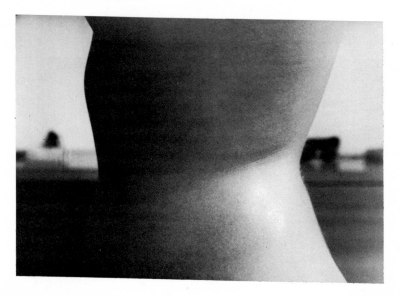

abstract in its effect: that is to say, it does not correspond to any dramatic or expressive necessity. This, to my mind, is no condemnation, though it will be for some. But Godard's subject-matter, his content, is strong enough, shall we say, to support any amount of abstraction he cares to impose on it.

A detailed analysis of this sequence would be far too complicated for a book of this sort. Suffice it to say that it is worked out so precisely that the camera is held on right and left of the screen much longer than it fixes on the centre; that the centre-held images are almost always equal in length to the time the camera takes in moving from right to centre or from centre to left. The same principle dominates a similar sequence in *Le Mépris*, in which Brigitte Bardot and Michel Piccoli are seated on either side of a table with a lamp between them. However, by making Piccoli switch the lamp on and off whenever the camera comes to rest on it in its ceaseless trip back and forth between the two people, Godard adds not only another visual element—the light going on and off—but also an aural one—the clicking of the switch.

This particular method of imposing abstraction on realistically shot material was to change after *Le Mépris*. In *Une Femme Mariée*, for example, he works rather towards a greater and greater splitting up of the shot, and then a re-pasting in a kind of collage technique which is sometimes formal, sometimes dramatically meaningful. "More and more with each film," he said in 1965, "it seems to me the greatest problem in filming is to decide where and why to begin a shot and where and why to end it." In keeping with this fragmented technique, the use of music also changes in *Une Femme Mariée*: all through the film he uses only three or four bars of Beethoven quartets; the music acts purely as punctuation. In *Made in U.S.A.* he will use just two chords from a symphony in the same way.

However, reality, the reality of the thing seen and shot, will always be respected. The one exception that springs to mind is that very beautiful scene in *Pierrot le Fou* in which Karina and Belmondo drive South through the night. We see a succession of red, yellow, and green traffic-lights reflected and flashing on the car's windscreen. But they are presented in too rhythmical a way possibly to be 'real'. Godard's explanation for the sequence is that he tried to re-create a sensation—the memory of traffic-lights flashing in the night—by playing with the elements that composed it. In other words, by what used to be called pure montage. However, adds Godard: "It's all right for a Michel Butor to cut up fragments of his verse in this way, but it's too *easy* to do in the cinema." By which he means, I suppose, that the image should be beautiful not because it is beautiful in itself but because it partakes of what he calls the "splendour of the true". (Actually, he's quoting both Plato and Rossellini.)

Perhaps the best example of the double pull towards both reality and abstraction can be found in *Masculin Féminin*. Looked at casually, this might be a television film; it appears to have been very simply shot, and its interest would seem to the casual observer to be almost entirely sociological or dramatic. To be sure, the basic story of Paul and Madeleine is constantly interrupted—if that is the word—by a number of incidents which bear no direct dramatic relation to the plot, but which do have an analogical function and value. The bystanders—the prostitute and her German client; the wife who shoots her husband; the man who sets fire to himself in front of the American hospital as a protest against the Vietnam War—all contribute to the general significance of the film. And I suppose the arbitrary introduction of these incidents could be seen as a kind of analogical method of narration which approaches the idea of abstraction.

But if one looks more carefully at the film, one can see, as much if not more than in the earlier films, Godard's specific techniques in play. It, too, is broken up into tableaux, only this time they are called *faits précis*. If we take two of these, numbers six and seven, we can get a good idea of how Godard works. Both are fairly similar in the sense that the first is set in the Bus Palladium, a dance-hall plus bowling-alley, arcade, etc., which was extremely popular in the winter of 1965, and the second is set in a launderette. Both tableaux last about 6 minutes. But each is treated in a totally different manner.

Masculin Féminin. Analogical incident: woman shoots man

Sequence six is composed entirely of four shots: the first is a brief street scene lasting 10 seconds; then we see the exterior of the Palladium for 7 seconds; the third shot shows the dance-floor for 18 seconds; the fourth and last shot is set in the arcade section and runs for 343 seconds, or about 5½ minutes. Yet this last is not a static dialogue scene, as one might imagine from its length. It could easily have been broken up into many short takes, for its subject-matter is extremely varied. One supposes at first that Godard has done it this way for convenience. The shot begins with Paul, Madeleine and Elizabeth at the bar; then the two girls leave, and a strange blonde girl comes up to Paul to ask him if he wants to have his picture taken with her. Why not, he says, and the camera follows them across the arcade, and waits outside an automatic-photo booth while we hear her offer him a picture of her breasts for 150 francs. Paul refuses, the curtain opens, and

Masculin Féminin. Analogical incident: Godard's version of *Dutchman*

he comes out, wanders around, and finally goes into a record-your-voice booth and records a lyrical expression of his love for Madeleine. He then takes a quick look at the bowling-alley, and the shot ends as a man rushes up to him, stabbing himself in the stomach. One might almost be back with Hitchcock and the 10-minute take.

Sequence seven could well have been treated in the same way. It begins with two exterior shots, one of Paul lasting 10 seconds, another an 11-second street scene. The third shot begins with Paul entering the launderette where he finds his friend Robert. The launderette sequence lasts 5½ minutes, just as did the Palladium shot; it consists entirely of Paul and his friend talking together. But rather than film it all in one take, Godard breaks it up into no fewer than fifteen shots ranging from 5 to 58 seconds each. There is no dramatic reason for doing this; or at least there is no more

Masculin Féminin. The Palladium Arcade (Jean-Pierre Léaud, Chantal Goya, Marlène Jobert) and the launderette (Jean-Pierre Léaud)

reason to fragment this scene than there was *not* to fragment the earlier one. So one can only conclude that this is another example of Godard's 'will to abstraction', as the Germans would call it, at work. Formally, the contrast between the two sequences is satisfying; and finally it is these formal considerations which succeed in giving the film the structure that it seems to lack, and which make it, in spite of its modest air, one of Godard's most achieved films.

This launderette sequence, however, is not the end of the tableau. It is followed by an extraordinary series of shots which point in the direction of Godard's most recent films. Their dramatic function is to act as a bridge between the launderette sequence in which Paul and his friend talk over political and social problems and the next tableau in which Paul and the three girls discuss sex.

It consists of six shots: all together they add up to 39 seconds. Quite unrealistically, they alternate between day and night. The first shot is inside a café at night: 5 seconds. The second is a daytime view of the street from the interior of a café: 6 seconds. The third tracks horizontally along a street at night: 7 seconds. The fourth is a street by day with a couple coming at the camera:

11 seconds. The fifth is a shop-window lit up at night: 5 seconds. The last is a daytime view of a street after the rain: 5 seconds.

This alternation of day and night is arbitrary, of course; but not completely so. First of all, the shots are of differing lengths, thus avoiding any feeling of rigidity. But, most important, what we hear on the soundtrack more or less parallels what we see. The first shot coincides exactly with an off-screen commentary by Paul. (Throughout the film the characters recite a kind of poetic counterpoint to the action.) Paul's words: "that night is lonely and terrible after which no day comes" are expressed by the café night scene. The second shot, daytime, corresponds to Catherine's words about how American scientists have succeeded in transmitting ideas from one brain to another by injection. Almost, but not quite, because just before her last words, we cut to the next night shot, over which we hear Robert's statement that it is not the conscience of men that determines their existence but their social condition which determines their conscience. Day returns with Elizabeth's statement that one might suppose that in twenty years time each citizen can carry around a little electric gadget that will give him sensations of pleasure and sexual satisfaction. But on the word pleasure we cut back to night, and Madeleine says "Give us this day our television"—and then we cut to the final day shot as she concludes: "and an automobile, but deliver us from freedom."

Now one could make out a case that Godard has treated this sequence dramatically. Darkness corresponds to Paul's loneliness, to Robert's pessimistic view of life and to Madeleine's plea for a television-set. Daytime would correspond to Catherine's rosy optimism about what science will be able to do and to Elizabeth's Utopian future in which sexual problems will be solved by gadget. But I think we must take it that such an idea is meant to be only very lightly suggested. To me, the interest of the sequence is that it shows Godard reaching towards that almost total escape from the *shot as filmed* that he will achieve in *Made in U.S.A.* and *Deux ou Trois Choses que je sais d'elle*. And it brings out even more strongly than before that dialectical tension between reality and abstraction which forms the basis of all of Godard's later films.

Or, putting it another way, Godard quotes Malraux's dictum: "Art is born like a fire, of what it burns." Just so, and Godard is fascinated by the possibility of capturing reality with the camera and then, and only then, doing something with it. And that something, of course, is to make of it a work of art. As he wrote about another film-maker: "His films are not a reflection of life; they are life itself made into film, and seen from behind the looking-glass from which the cinema captures life." Godard has gone on record as having said that there is no progress in art . . . only change. "Between Chardin and Braque, there is not so much difference. Some, but not so much." Perhaps that was true. But just as there is a fundamental difference between Braque and, say, Lichtenstein, so there is between the cinema before Godard and the cinema after Godard. Perhaps not progress, but a fundamental change. Such fundamental changes in art would seem to be a characteristic of the twentieth century. Or is it simply that they *seem* fundamental to us? If God (or Henri Langlois) could edit Lumière and Méliès together, mightn't he get something like Godard?

For those who feel that an obsession with pure form is somehow wrong, one can, in Godard's defence, quote—of all people—Leon Trotsky. The following paragraph comes from an essay which is supposed to be *against* the Russian Formalists, but which makes out one of the best cases for the importance of form in art, as well as for the importance of the random, aleatory, or chance elements. (Change the word 'verbal' to 'visual' to make it applicable to Godard.)

"In its striving towards artistic materialisation, a subjective idea will be stimulated and jolted by form and may sometimes be pushed on to a path which was entirely unforeseen. This simply means that verbal form is *not* a passive reflection of a preconceived artistic idea, but an active element which influences the idea itself. But such an active mutual relationship —in which form influences and at times entirely transforms content—is known to us in all fields of social and even biological life."

MARINA VLADY
DANS
UN FILM DE
JEAN-LUC GODARD
deux ou trois choses
que je sais d'elle...
RAOUL COUTARD
Production ANOUCHKA FILMS • ARGOS FILMS • LES FILMS DU CARROSSE • PARC FILM
Eastmancolor • Techniscope
AJAX
nouveau LESSIVE
PREMIER PRIX
20 ans

Chapter Five

Godard's two most recent films (May 1967) require special treatment, not only because they are the newest, but because they are a kind of summing up of his work till now. *Made in U.S.A.* takes certain tendencies further than ever—perhaps too far, as we shall see—and *Deux ou Trois Choses que je sais d'elle* is, for me, the greatest of Godard's films. Furthermore, although they were not conceived originally as a diptych, he would have liked them to be shown together on the same night in the same cinema. This was not possible, as each has a different producer; nor has it yet been possible for him to try out another idea, one modelled on Faulkner's *The Wild Palms*: that is, to play both films simultaneously, as it were, with a reel of *Made in U.S.A.* alternating with a reel of *Deux ou Trois Choses que je sais d'elle* and so forth, just as Faulkner alternated chapters of *The Old Man* and *The Wild Palms*.

While Godard was working on the preparations for *Deux ou Trois Choses que je sais d'elle*, he was approached by Georges de Beauregard, who had produced *A Bout de Souffle*, *Le Petit Soldat*, *Les Carabiniers*, *Pierrot le Fou*, and, in part, *Le Mépris*. Beauregard had suffered severe financial losses as a result of not having been able to show *La Religieuse*, banned by the Gaullist Minister of Information. He proposed that Godard should make a film for him, cheaply and quickly, as, he said, only Godard knew how: a simple story film which would help to put Beauregard on his feet again. Godard accepted the idea, partly to help out an old friend,

Made in USA: Anna Karina in Atlantic City and with radio car

partly because the challenge of making two films at once excited him. During that summer of 1966, Howard Hawks's *The Big Sleep* had been revived at an art house in Paris, and Godard tells us that he conceived the idea of a sort of remake, with Anna Karina—trench-coat and all—playing the detective who is trying to unravel an impenetrable mystery. "It's going to be a real story film," he declared at the time. The result was something else again.

First of all, the connection with *The Big Sleep* is rather vague, and indeed may have been something of a blind, for the basic plot of the original conception of the film seems to have come from another source—an American novel published in the *Série Noire* of which Beauregard had bought the rights. That novel appears to have resembled *Kiss Me Deadly* more than *The Big Sleep*, and a scenario—eighteen pages long—was cooked up by Godard to raise money on. But it only vaguely resembles the finished film. It was called *The Secret*, and its heroine comes to a small town in France, only to discover that her lover has just died mysteriously, and that three or four people are very anxious to find certain papers which contain a secret he alone knew. By the end of the film, the heroine is convinced that the secret does not exist, that there were no papers. But the intrigue resembles, as I said earlier, *Kiss Me Deadly*, if one can imagine that film without its denouement, its mystery unsolved.

So much for the genesis of the work. The finished film of *Made in U.S.A.* has as its double theme the murder of Ben Barka and the assassination of Kennedy. Metaphorically, to be sure, and there are elements from the history of the whole post-war period—the Moroccan War, the Algerian situation, Agadir, the Fifth Republic.

On a first viewing, the plot is extremely confusing. Indeed, only after three screenings and with the help of a dialogue list, was I really able to follow it in detail. The reason for this confusion is quite simple: Godard's desire for realism. Nobody knows to this day who killed Ben Barka and how it was done; nobody knows for sure how or whether Figon, chief witness in the affair, was 'suicided'. And, Warren Report or not, no one yet knows the full story of the Kennedy assassination. Any film about these events which even presented a coherent story, let alone offered a solution, would, according to Godard, be false and dishonest. Just as *Les Carabiniers* seemed to many stupid and nonsensical, so *Made in U.S.A.* seems to many confused and absurd. The reasons are similar in both cases. But at least anyone could *follow Les Carabiniers*, whereas the same is not true of *Made in U.S.A.* Godard's justification for this confusion lies in the impossibility of our understanding some aspects of both the Kennedy assassination and the Ben Barka affair. The following report from the *New York Times* gives better than anything else an idea of the plot of *Made in U.S.A.*

"Mr. Ferrie, who was found dead yesterday, was a major figure in an investigation by the New Orleans District Attorney, James Garrison, of an alleged plot to assassinate President Kennedy. . . . Mr. Martin told the Assistant District Attorney shortly after the assassination that Mr. Ferrie knew Oswald, that he trained the President's assassin in the use of rifles with telescopic sights, and that Mr. Ferrie had visited Dallas about two weeks before the assassination of the President. Documents disclosed yesterday that Martin had admitted to the Secret Service and the F.B.I. that his story was a lie.

"On the night of Nov. 29, 1963, two Secret Service Agents . . . interviewed Mr. Martin 'at length' in his apartment in New Orleans. Their report states: 'Martin, who has every appearance of being an alcoholic, admitted during the interview that he suffers from telephonitis when drinking, and that it was during one of his drinking bouts that . . . he told this fantastic story about Ferrie being involved with Oswald.'" (22 February 1967.)

Now, *Made in U.S.A.*: Paula Nelson comes to 'Atlantic City' to find her lover Richard; on arrival she learns that he is dead. A number of people with mysterious motives try to join forces with her, but she is concerned chiefly with discovering Richard's assassin. In the course of her searches, she gets mixed up with the police, gangsters, and the 'police parallèle'.

The existence of these private police forces was one of the revelations of the Ben Barka affair, and the whole atmosphere of a police state permeates Atlantic City, which in spite of the name is supposed to be a town somewhere in the French provinces, although the film was actually shot in the western suburbs of Paris. The action is set in 1969, and Richard is modelled on Figon. Paula comes out of the affair having killed at least three men, and not really having discovered who murdered Richard. It may even be that he was killed in a purely private quarrel about a girl. Dramatically speaking, Godard continually cuts the ground from under our feet: the one sure idea one has is that Paula is the heroine; by the end, we are not so sure even of that. She may be no better than her victims.

The plot is difficult to follow not only because of the lack of information about the characters and their true motives, but even more because of the technique of narration Godard adopts. Here he pushes fragmentation almost as far as it can go: the narrative elements are analysed into tiny movements, and then recomposed, somewhat in the manner of classical Cubist paintings. Not systematically: there are long sequences, even longish takes; but in between these sequences, the transitions are treated almost abstractly. For example, the first two reels show us Paula at her hotel in Atlantic City, the encounter with the first of the gangsters and her subsequent meeting with his nephew and the nephew's Japanese girl-friend. Paula knocks out the gangster, Monsieur Typhus; the Japanese girl sings a song in some unknown language which doesn't sound like Japanese; Paula and the nephew, called David Goodis,* have a long conversation about everything except the death of Richard; the sequence ends with her asking him to help her, but not to tell anything to the police; and finally she leaves, gliding across the screen from right to left.

Then follows an almost impenetrable sequence of seventeen brief shots: (1) A poster with the name of Jean Jaurès (famous Socialist leader who was assassinated on the eve of the First World War)—Paula moves across it continuing the right to left movement of the previous shot and disappears: 29 seconds. (2) Paula in front of a bright red wall, swinging her hair in luscious arabesques: 5 seconds. (3) A girl in a yellow dress starts to put on a white nurse's smock: 5 seconds. (4) Paula in front of the red wall: 3 seconds. (5) Paula, her position reversed, against the same red wall: 1 second. (6) Paula back in her previous pose against the wall: 1 second. (7) Paula disappearing out of frame on the left leaving the red wall: 7 seconds. (8) Girl in the smock going towards a door: on the soundtrack we hear Paula's second commentary: "Is it really you that I'm going to find dead, oh Richard, oh my king? In what

---

* He is named after the author of *Down There*, from which Truffaut's *Tirez sur le Pianiste* was adapted.

second-rate tragedy are you again making me play a new role?": 21 seconds. (9) The camera moves down a white wall into black to discover Paula seated, putting cartridges into a gun which she then hides in a hollowed-out copy of the *Larousse Cookbook*. The camera tilts up and down on her as she fluffs out her hair: 30 seconds. (10) The girl in the smock begins to talk, but we do not hear what she says, we only see her lips move: 20 seconds. (11) Paula pushes her way into what seems to be a dentist's office brandishing her gun; she speaks, but again we do not hear her voice: 19 seconds. (12) We see a body seated in the dentist's chair with the head wrapped in gauze. (13) Gun in hand, Paula unwinds the gauze, to discover a terrifying flayed head: 16 seconds. (14) Paula outside against a red door, and the third commentary begins: "Fortunately I had become a brunette, and Professor Korvo did not recognise the blonde student from Agadir": 6 seconds. (15) Begins with the word 'recognise' of the commentary and we are in the street in front of a house with yellow and blue shutters; Paula passes across the screen from left to right: 6 seconds. (16) We see a strange red-brick building, and then M. Typhus, the gangster Paula knocked out, chases her up an external staircase: 5 seconds. (17) A shot of the electric signs on the Champs-Elysées, over which we suddenly hear the voice of Marianne Faithfull singing "It is the evening of the day". End of sequence.

Even breaking down the sequence in this way does not clarify what is supposed to be going on, and when one sees the film for the first time, one is almost totally mystified. It's rather like a mosaic gone wild, one which is composed of such tiny tessera that the figure does not emerge. It is only by analysing the sequence on the movieola that one begins to be able to make something of it, although it must be admitted that such a sequence does have an effect on the viewer even without his fully understanding it. But, judging from Godard's next film, he was to come to a realisation that the fragmentation/collage method is best applied, not to narration, but to something else. For to narrate an incomprehensible plot in this difficult manner would seem to compound unnecessarily the problems placed before the viewer.

107

Made in USA: the sequence →

4

5

6

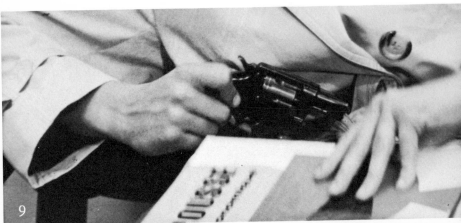

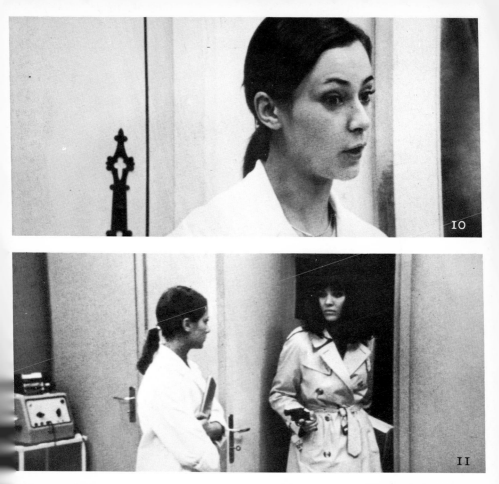

10

11

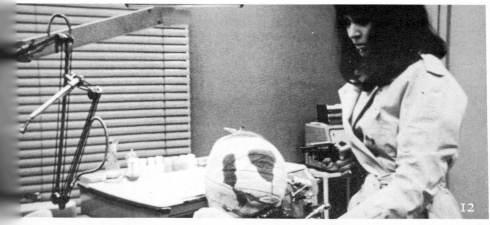

12

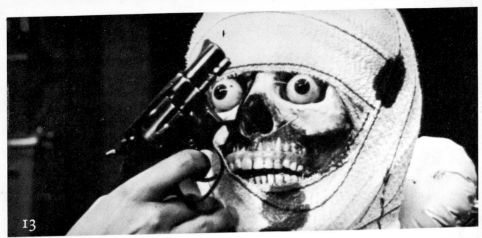

13

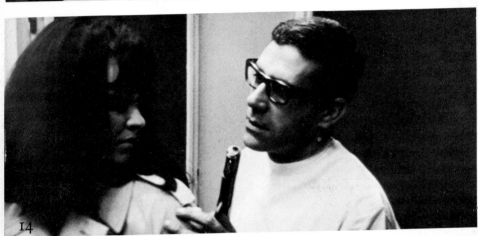

14

15

Made in USA: the sequence described on pages 106–7

But that is not all: the soundtrack of *Made in U.S.A.* also presents obstacles. The man Paula is looking for is, we are told by Godard, Richard Politzer. But one never hears his last name in the film: whenever a character begins to pronounce it, he gets no further than the first syllable and his voice is drowned out by the noise of a passing jet or an automobile. Then, too, there are long passages of the film in which we listen to an almost completely incomprehensible tape-recording of Richard's voice. Wilfully so, for when Paula later records a message herself on the same machine, we can hear it perfectly. Richard's tapes are a collage of political speeches, and of course we are not supposed to understand every word—just to get a jumbled impression of jumbled speeches. Nevertheless, it is a painful experience, and one which can enrage an audience.

Furthermore, *Made in U.S.A.* pushes the antiphonal commentaries of *Pierrot le Fou* one logical step further. In that film, Belmondo and Karina sometimes took one line of commentary each, alternating with the other; one could just about put it all together. Here, at one point, Paula and Widmark each have a commentary which they deliver absolutely *simultaneously*, making it impossible really to understand either one.

The use of music, too, is carried much further than in the earlier films. Fragments of Beethoven and Schumann are used: the introductory theme of the Largo of Schumann's Fourth Symphony emerges as a kind of hopeful leitmotif; and some piano music appears at other places. But most extraordinary is Godard's systematic punctuation—and there is no other word—of the film by a tiny passage from a Beethoven symphony which consists of two loud chords, the second of which is prolonged a second or two by strings alone: something like 'bang BANGggggg'. But noises are also used in this punctuating manner—the sound of the jets appears not only when Politzer's name is about to be mentioned, but also often immediately follows the two chords or the piano fragment.

The sense of the absurd that Godard is seeking is heightened by various extraneous interruptions, like the Japanese girl's incomprehensible song, Marianne Faithfull's rendition of "It is the evening of the day", Laszlo Szabo's imitation of Sylvester and Tweetie Pie which we already heard in *Le Grand Escroc*. Most infuriating of all to some people, the whole of reel three is devoted to an Hegelian discussion in a bar: "The glass is not in my wine, the barman is in the pocket of the jacket of his pencil; the floor stubs itself against the cigarette," etc. It does have a point, of course, as the ending of this long litany makes clear: "I am what you are, he is not what we are; they are what you are, he has what they have." Paula and the police are inextricably linked—they are one, even, because they are both manifestations of a general situation. "Right and left are a completely outmoded equation," we are told ". . . one must learn to pose the problem differently." And the film ends with Paula's question: "Well, how?"

The main difficulty with *Made in U.S.A.*, it seems to me, is that Godard has chosen to do two things in one film—to push forward his anti-narrative techniques and fragmentation of plot to reach the absurd, and at the same time to set out an exposition of the absurdity of the world in which we live. The two would seem to go together very well. In fact, according to traditional views of aesthetics, it is wholly proper to have the form express the content. But this has not been Godard's way before, and it doesn't work too well here. He is at his most effective when the two are working against each other: here they are almost tautologically the same. In his next film, he was not to make the same mistake; if in fact it was a mistake.

Before going on to *Deux ou Trois Choses que je sais d'elle*, I should say that I have perhaps been as unfair to *Made in U.S.A.* as I was to *Pierrot le Fou*. Both films, taken in isolation, are remarkable achievements, and both are visually extremely beautiful. I have doubtless allowed my preferences for the films which immediately succeeded them—*Masculin Féminin* and *Deux ou Trois Choses que je sais d'elle*—to emphasise unduly the weaknesses of *Pierrot le Fou* and *Made in U.S.A.* Or is it perhaps simply that my general argument applies less to these two films than to the others? I hope not, but it may well be.

Deux ou Trois Choses que je sais d'elle: Vance Packard and *Elle*

Deux ou Trois Choses que je sais d'elle is, in Godard's own words, a sociological essay in the form of a novel but written, not with words, but with notes of music. It is much more ambitious than *Made in U.S.A.*, both in its subject-matter, which deals with the whole Parisian region—the 'her' of the title—and in its form. "At this moment," wrote Godard, "the whole area round Paris is being reorganised. On a vast scale, the region is being transformed; and what strikes me is that it is really being rearranged as a huge brothel. One finds here all the things that characterise the brothel: the inhabitants are obedient and docile, and they are prostituting themselves. If I have filmed a prostitute, it is because I wanted to show this. I mean, I could have filmed a worker or a technician who, three-quarters of the time, doesn't behave, *grosso modo*, any differently." In short, the film is a kind of apotheosis of Godard's feelings about prostitution in modern life.

Deux ou Trois Choses que je sais d'elle: Marina Vlady

The idea came from an exposé in *Le Nouvel Observateur* which showed how many of the women residing in the new low-cost high-rise housing complexes resort to casual prostitution in order to make ends meet. The practice has become so common, apparently, that there is even a name for them: 'shooting stars'. The economic reasons for this, as Godard explained in an interview, are that most of these women have been forcibly re-located in these dreary buildings outside the city. Their flats are modern, with central heating and all modern conveniences, but they are not allowed to bring with them their old furniture—for fear of woodworm—and so they have the initial expense of refurnishing the house. Then there is the cost of moving, charges for connecting gas and light, and furthermore many of them, carried away by their new-found luxury, run up heavy bills for gas and electricity. From the very beginning they are in debt. Faced with the necessity of paying off these debts, and more important, affording all the luxuries with which our consumer society tempts us, many of these women go into Paris (some once a week, some only at the difficult end of the month), to prostitute themselves. Returning home with a full grocery bag, they are much appreciated for their 'clever management' by their unsuspecting—or complaisant—husbands.

This is the pretext for the film, and it also gives it a basic structure: twenty-four hours in the day of one of these 'shooting stars', an attractive young housewife (played by Marina Vlady) who lives with her garage mechanic husband and their two children in a housing complex. The film begins one evening and ends the next, during which time she has spent the day in Paris. . . .

But here, more than in Godard's previous films, prostitution is only a pretext: it is integrated into a much larger social picture. Godard's view is that under the pretence of reforming and modernising social structures in France, the Gaullist régime is only trying to regularise, to standardise the natural tendencies of capitalism. He deduces further that by systematising its *dirigisme* and centralisation, the government is accentuating still further the distortion of the national economy, and even more that of the everyday morality which is its basis. "This film," he states, "is a continuation of the movement begun by Resnais in *Muriel*: an attempt at a description of a phenomenon known in mathematics and sociology as a 'complex'. If this young woman lives in what is called a housing complex, it is not only a play on words. Therefore I sought to link the manner in which she arranges her life with the way in which the government's *Plan* is arranging the region of Paris."

In some ways this film resembles *Alphaville*, in that both have a kind of master idea behind them, one which helps give them unity and strength. Furthermore, one could say that *Deux ou Trois Choses que je sais d'elle* shows us the Alphaville of today. But technically and formally speaking, it is more like a successful remake of *Une Femme Mariée*. That film was characterised by Godard as an attempt "to consider subjects as objects, a film in which chases would alternate with ethnological interviews, where the spectacle of life would be finally blended with an analysis of life: in short, a free film."

Deux ou Trois Choses que je sais d'elle is in one sense freer than *Une Femme Mariée*, but because of its general context it is at the same time more controlled, more systematically worked out. It is perhaps not quite exact to say that subjects are treated as objects: in this film subjects and objects are of almost equal importance. The shots, for example, of the cranes on the building sites which constantly reappear throughout the film are just as important as the images of the heroine. "Objects exist, and if one pays more attention to them than to people, it is precisely because they exist more than these people. Dead objects are still alive. Living people are often already dead."

His model, in some respects, has been Francis Ponge, a French poet who began during the last war to write little poems in prose which are neither more nor less than the descriptions of objects: the book was called by the untranslatable title of *Le Parti Pris des Choses*—or, roughly, *The Things' Side of It*. In Ponge's view, the poet should pay as much attention to a bar of soap, a pebble, or a goldfish, as to ideas, emotions, or morals: all explicitly banished in a puritanical insistence that the poet's job is a glorification of anything and everything. Philosophically speaking, his work was bound to appeal to the Existentialists, and in fact Sartre did much to make him better known. Ponge himself suggests his work to be of importance in its attempt to strip poetry bare of its accretions, to return to the basic job of the poet: the 'naming of things'. Curiously enough, another of his ideas—that the manner in which a soap-bubble explodes, or an egg develops, can tell us much about the universe—has gained increased validity since the atomic revolution of 1945. And when Godard shows us for what seems like two or three minutes a shot of a coffee-cup seen from above, with the bubbles first gradually separating, then re-forming into a circle in the centre, then redispersing, one feels one is experiencing something much more important than at first sight it seems to be. Just what, it is difficult to say. The music of the spheres? The movement of molecules?

The many shots of cranes, steam-shovels, dump trucks are of course easier to 'justify'—they are what is physically transforming the new Paris, and the way in which they tower over the old Paris dominating the life of the inhabitants is thematically quite clear. So, too, the shots of consumer products, which, as in *Une Femme Mariée*, are meant to figure the role of advertising in our lives. But the coffee-cup, and another extraordinarily long-held shot of the end of a burning cigarette, carry more premonitory weight than one would have thought possible, thus no doubt justifying Ponge's belief that anything, properly considered, is a worthy subject for the poet. Or, as William Carlos Williams put it, "No ideas but in things."

Before going on to Godard's use of subjective descriptions, one must point out that the characters of the film are also seen as objects:

"It is 4:45.
Should I speak of Juliette or of these leaves?
Since it is impossible, in any case, really to do both together, let's say that both tremble gently in this beginning of the end of an October afternoon."

Every attempt is continually made to remind us that we are watching a film—nowhere can one slip back into simply absorbing a story. At the very beginning, we are told by the narrator (Godard himself, whispering): "This woman is Marina Vlady. She is an actress. She's wearing a midnight-blue sweater with two yellow stripes. She is of Russian origin, and her hair is dark chestnut or light brown, I'm not sure which." Then Marina Vlady takes up the commentary herself and says: "Yes, to speak as if one were quoting truth. It was old Brecht who said that actors should seem to be quoting." Then Godard takes it up again: "This woman is Juliette Janson. She lives here. She is wearing a midnight-blue sweater with two yellow stripes. Her hair is dark chestnut or else light brown. I am not sure which. She is of Russian origin." And then Marina Vlady, assuming her character, says: "Two years ago, I was in Martinique . . ." and we're off. But this is not just a stylistic trick: throughout the film, whenever one might forget one is watching a film, one is caught up short by Godard. In any case, there are also Godard's own commentaries, such as the one that follows the first long dramatic scene. "It is certain that the rearranging of the Parisian area is going to make it easier for the government to pursue its class politics, and for the great monopolies to orient and organise the economy without worrying too much about the needs and aspirations to a better life of the eight million people who live here."

Curiously enough, the effect is not to destroy the dramatic scenes; rather I found that they were heightened and given, not only more meaning (which one would expect), but also more beauty by being thus set off.

Now for what Godard has called the 'subjectively descriptive' side of the film. In an attempt to make his mosaic full and meaningful, and in accordance with his basic idea that if you have something to say, the best way is just to say it, many of the characters interrupt their dialogue to let us hear—straight to camera—their thoughts. Even minor characters—attendants in shops—while moving across the room to get a dress, will stop, face the camera and say things like: "I stop work at seven o'clock. I've got a date at eight with Jean-Claude. We'll go to a restaurant, and then to the cinema." Or in the beauty parlour, one of the girls suddenly turns and says: "My name is Paulette Cadjaris. I failed at being a shorthand typist. No, I don't believe in the future . . . I walk a lot; I don't like to be closed in. When I can, I read. The cinema—two or three times a month, but never in the summer. I've never been to the theatre. But I'd like to. . . ." It is almost as if they were answering an invisible interviewer, which is doubtless exactly what they are doing. But sometimes the interruptions are briefer, more spontaneous, as if somehow a layer of personality has been lifted off, and one plunges for a second beneath the depths of ordinary conversation, and the character 'justifies' himself, somewhat in the manner of a Noh play.

In the café, for example, where Juliette meets some of her fellow part-time prostitutes, there is the following exchange: JULIETTE:

Deux ou Trois Choses que je sais d'elle: Marina Vlady →

"Hello, how are things?" FRIEND: "All right. I'm waiting here for Jean-Paul." JULIETTE: "Me, I'll be here until tonight." FRIEND: "Oh, you've got a new pair of shoes. I live in that large block near the Autoroute du Sud. I come to Paris twice a month. You know, those big blue and white buildings." And then the conversation continues. Sometimes these interruptions simply provide information about the speaker which relates him or her to the general situation. At other times one feels that a soul has been stripped before us.

Juliette swings throughout the film from conversation to her own thoughts—or occasionally to Godard speaking through her mouth. But the practice differs from that of *Strange Interlude*, in which the whole point was the contrast between what the characters 'said' and what they 'thought'. Here there is no contrast, rather a deeper penetration and a generalising. For example, early in the film, Juliette's husband comes into the kitchen to announce that their friend Roger is going home. Juliette replies, "Right, I'm coming," and then, without any gear switching, she immediately continues her thoughts from earlier in the scene: "You try often to find, to analyse the meaning of words, but one is too easily impressed by them. You've got to admit that nothing is simpler than thinking that this or that thing is just a matter of course."

Or later, in the by-the-hour hotel where she takes a young worker, she jumps from a discussion of what they are going to do to a general reflection: "It's not my fault if I've got a passive side. To have sexual relations. I don't see why I should be ashamed to be a woman. . . . Perhaps I should leave Robert. He doesn't want to get ahead in life. He is always happy with what he's got. In Martinique it was already like that. . . ."

One might think that this mixture of commentary, internal monologue, ordinary dialogue, the lengthy examination of objects, the brief flashes of the cranes and the bulldozers, would make the film very difficult to follow. And yet it doesn't. First of all, we are given a thread to hang on to—a day in the life of Juliette Janson. And then that day is, as it were, blocked out. We begin after dinner in her flat. The next morning Juliette sets off for Paris, leaving her child in the care of a little old man who uses his meagrely furnished flat as a kind of nursery-cum-brothel. (In one room he looks after the children, telling them fairy-tales; while another he rents out by the half-hour to couples who have nowhere else to go. Everyone pays in tinned goods.) The next sections show Juliette at a dress shop, then in the bar where the prostitutes hang out. Next, there is a long scene at a smart hotel where Juliette and a friend take care of a rich American client, just back from Vietnam. (John Bogus, war correspondent in Saigon for an Arkansas daily, is played by the late Raoul Lévy in a curious mixture of accented English and French, as he puts forth the curious reflection that since one dead Vietcong costs the Americans a million dollars, President Johnson could easily afford to have 20,000 whores for himself instead.) From there we go to her hairdresser, to Robert's garage, then to a café where Robert awaits Juliette, and then home again.

These nine 'chapters' help to give the work a kind of shape. Much more important, however, is the fact that the flash-shots and the sudden interruptions are not, as in *Made in U.S.A.*, bits of *narration*. Therefore we never worry about deciphering them—we don't have to. They can simply act on us symbolically, and this makes them much easier to absorb. In *Made in U.S.A.*, these 2-second shots advanced the plot; here they simply fill out the ensemble, the complex. *Made in U.S.A.* took Godard's experiments with form and narration further than he had gone before; but because there is a coherent master idea behind *Deux ou Trois Choses que je sais d'elle* it succeeds on all levels. Content and form are played off one against the other in an entirely satisfying and rewarding way, each one pushing the other forward to give the film a strength and an impetus that makes it for me the summit of Godard's work.

However, precisely because this film brings to a head all of Godard's ideas or obsessions about contemporary society—prostitution, modern living, the consumer society—one must examine it a little more closely. How relevant is this idea? Or, to put it more crudely, how *true* is it? Those who disagree point out that whatever he may say, it is certainly true that the average person has a better life now in our American-orientated consumer society than he ever did before. People work less; there is Social Security. Godard can say what he likes about people prostituting themselves for automobiles; surely it is better that workers should have holidays by the sea than not. And although sacrifices might be made to get a washing-machine, isn't it better than slaving over a hot tub? Doesn't nylon keep poor mothers from darning socks all the time; and could nylon exist and be as cheap as it is were it not for advertising and the whole set-up of Western society? Is it wrong for advertising to excite desires people would not otherwise have had? Is not desire the motivating force of life? Rather than complain about the vulgarity of television, should not Godard reflect on how it has enriched the lives of many people living in the country, far from all other sources of information or culture?

All these objections to Godard's philosophy have a certain degree of validity. Supposing for a moment that one agreed with his opponents, could one still maintain that Godard was none the less a great film-maker? One could always weasel out of the question by saying that it doesn't matter what an artist thinks; everything depends on how he expresses it. Or one could take W. H. Auden's line that poets will be forgiven all their stupidities because of their talent: that Time

> Worships language and forgives
> Everyone by whom it lives . . .
> Time that with this strange excuse
> Pardoned Kipling and his views,
> And will pardon Paul Claudel,
> Pardons him for writing well.

Although it appears that Auden has cut these lines from the most recent edition of his poems, they obviously still have a certain validity. But I don't think one has to resort to an art for art's sake viewpoint with Godard—he'd hate it, anyhow. And I don't think he is naïve enough to want to throw away all the progress of the twentieth century. However, although one can say that prostitution on every level has always existed, it is certainly true that in recent years it is greatly on the upswing in France. It may be a purely local phenomenon, although I doubt if there are really local phenomena in this second half of the twentieth century. And to say, as does Godard's arch-enemy, *Madame Express*, that things are going the same way in Russia is, in Godard's eyes, no excuse. True enough, in *Deux ou Trois Choses que je sais d'elle* there is a conversation between a girl and a 'Nobel Prize winner' in which she asks him what the morality of Communism will be. He replies that it will be much the same as it is now. What, then, will be the difference, she asks? And the only reply she gets is that under Communism it will be easier to explain.

But this Nobel Prize winner is called Ivanoff—a Russian; it has become quite clear in the past year or so that Godard tends to lump the Russians in with the Americans as being tarred with the same capitalistic brush. It would seem also that he looks upon the Chinese cultural revolution with increasing favour. And one knows that his latest film is called *La Chinoise*, and is about a pro-Chinese Communist girl at the Sorbonne and her struggles with the old-line Moscow-orientated Communists.

For many people this will doubtless be enough to dismiss Godard for ever. How *can* he, one can hear them wail. And yet, *pace* Shelley, poets are *not* the unacknowledged legislators of the world. Their function is not to solve our problems but to make us aware that we've got problems.

> "I am doing nothing other than seeking reasons to live happily . . .
> A new world in which both men and things will have harmonious relations.
> That is my aim.
> It is ultimately as much political as poetic.
> It explains, in any case, the rage for expression,
> Of whom? Of me.
> Writer and painter."

Perhaps Godard has exaggerated the evils of our society; or perhaps the French have simply been afflicted with the most unpleasant expression of them—all the evils of a benevolent or not-so-benevolent dictatorship combined with the worst excesses of monopoly capitalism. But it doesn't matter whether the French experience awaits us all, or whether, as is more likely, it is an exaggerated and exacerbated expression of a more general state of affairs. Godard is doing his job as an artist in calling our attention to what he finds wrong in his society. It is up to us to decide whether he is right; or even if he is right, whether anything can be done about it. Are its evils a necessary corollary of the forty-hour week, paid vacations, and greater leisure time? It may well be so.

But also, one must recognise a deeper strain of pessimism in Godard which applies not only to economic and social factors, but to life itself. Juliette, alone in her bedroom, muses: "To define oneself in a single word: Not yet dead." An older woman in the beauty parlour suddenly speaks from the depths of her soul—and perhaps Godard's too: "I am very careful crossing streets. I think of the accident before it can happen. And that my life might stop right there . . . Unemployment . . . Sickness . . . Old Age . . . Death . . . Never . . . I have no plans for the future, for my horizons are closed."

These are problems that will not be solved no matter what form of society one lives in; not even Mao Tse-tung has a solution. Just before the end of the film, when Robert and Juliette return to their flat, Robert says:

"Well, here at last." Juliette replies: "Where?" ROBERT: "Home." JULIETTE: "And then what, what are we going to do?" ROBERT: "Sleep . . . what's got into you?" JULIETTE: "And then what?" ROBERT: "We'll get up." JULIETTE: "And then what?" ROBERT: "The same thing. We'll start all over again. We'll wake up, work, eat." JULIETTE: "And then what?" ROBERT: "I dunno . . . Die." JULIETTE: "And then what?" And as she pronounces those last words we get a flash of a petrol-pump, its dial immobile; then it begins to turn slowly, and then faster and faster. The figures whirl by in an obscene parody of life.

Of course, this Beckettian view of life—we are born astride the grave—is not incompatible with an interest in social progress. But it does help to give us a perspective on Godard's view of society, and above all it makes us aware that Godard is speaking in general terms of the problems of life. He is not giving us a recipe for a better life; that is not his job. But he is enriching our understanding of it. Like many artists, he is a reformer: it is up to us to decide how practical are his reforms, how much we are willing to sacrifice to achieve a healthier state of society. He is both contesting the conditions under which we live, and at the same time restating the human condition. Equally important, he is contesting the way in which films are made, by continually reinventing the cinema.

Godard's characters often quote Lenin's statement that Ethics are the Aesthetics of the future. But Godard himself wrote: "It may be true that one has to choose between ethics and aesthetics, but it is no less true that whichever one chooses, one will always find the other at the end of the road. For the very definition of the human condition should be in the *mise en scène* itself."

"Literary critics," said Godard, "often praise works like *Ulysses* or *Fin de Partie* because they exhaust a certain genre, they close the doors on it. But in the cinema we are always praising works which *open* doors." Let us now praise Godard, then, who has opened so many.

Chapter Six

It was difficult to predict in which direction Godard would move after that summing-up of his career in *Deux ou Trois Choses*; all one could say with certainty was that he would not stand still. Nor has he. In the three years since *Deux ou Trois Choses* his work has undergone a radical transformation. Just as *Masculin Féminin*, *Made in U.S.A.* and *Deux ou Trois Choses* formed a kind of trilogy, each commenting on a different facet of contemporary life, so *La Chinoise*, *Weekend* and *Le Gai Savoir* form another, very different kind of trilogy. Three factors have determined Godard's recent development. First, of course, is his increased interest in, and commitment to, politics. Secondly, following from this, a more total abandon of fictional forms and, concurrently, a flight from the romanticism which informed his earlier work. Thirdly, his second marriage, to Anne Wiazemsky.

The polite convention when writing about contemporary figures is largely to ignore their private life. And yet it is clear that this may have a significant relation to their work. One need only compare the films Godard made while married to Anna Karina with those after their divorce to see this. However, it is sometimes difficult to say whether the artist's private life has influenced his work, or, perhaps, vice versa. But the fact that Anne Wiazemsky is much younger than Godard is surely of importance. When Godard made *Masculin Féminin*, it was avowedly as a 'tourist', an older man spending a month with his juniors. In *La Chinoise*,

La Chinoise: "Behind the limpid eyes of Véronique . . ."

however, he seems to have adopted almost totally the point of view of his protagonists.

So accurately did Godard gauge the mood of a certain sector of youth, that the film clearly can be seen as an anticipation of the events that were to overtake France in the month of May, 1968—a year later. At the time *La Chinoise* was first shown, however, many people were convinced that it bore little relation to contemporary realities. At the Venice Festival, one of the jurors, a Frenchwoman who had children of university age, was left-wing herself, and lived bang in the middle of the future scene of the revolt, declared to her fellow-jurors that, although she too admired the film, they must all understand that it was a kind of fantasy, that nothing like that could actually take place in France: there were no students like those of *La Chinoise*. Either she was wrong, or else Nature really did imitate Art.

Consider: the film describes the life of a group of young people who during one summer try to apply to their own lives the theoretical and practical methods of Mao Tse-tung, the methods in whose name he broke with the *embourgeoisement* of the Russians, as well as that of the principal Eastern European Communist parties. For them, the most important event of the past ten years has been the growing opposition between the Chinese and the Russian views of Communism.

The five characters represent, as did those in Gorki's *Lower Depths*, five different levels of society. They share a flat which has been lent to one of them by a friend whose parents are away for the summer. Véronique (Anne Wiazemsky) is a student at the Faculty of Nanterre, that new division of the Sorbonne located in the desolate western suburbs of the city. She is destined to be a teacher and, for her, moral and intellectual problems are posed in immediate and concrete terms. Guillaume (Jean-Pierre Léaud) is an actor: in his case, Mao has led him to the path of a truly Socialist theatre. Henri (Michel Séméniako) is the most scientifically oriented of the five: he works at the Institute for Economic Logic. Kirilov (Lex de Bruijn) is named after the character in Dostoievsky's *The Possessed*: he is a painter, and his task is to paint the slogans on the walls of the flat, e.g. "We must confront vague ideas with clear images", "Socialist art died at Brest-Litovsk", or "A minority with the correct revolutionary line is no longer a minority". Yvonne (Juliet Berto) represents the peasant class. She came to Paris as a char, slipped into prostitution, and was 'saved' by Henri and the others; her job is to cook and clean for the group.

The first title in the film is "Un film en train de se faire", and indeed *La Chinoise* is very much a film in the making. There are only tiny elements of plot: the first half of the film presents the characters, first separately, then in little groups. The second half is somewhat more dramatic: Véronique proposes the assassination of an important person in the French cultural world. They all agree with the idea, except Henri who still defends the notion of peaceful co-existence with the bourgeoisie. He is therefore excluded from the group for revisionism. Kirilov commits suicide, haunted by thoughts of death and by the Dostoievskian proposition which he translates into Marxist terms—if Marxism-Leninism exists, then all is permitted: therefore I can kill myself. It is Véronique, significantly, who is left to carry out the assassination, and equally significantly she bungles it and ends up killing two people instead. The Marxist-Leninist vacation is over; it was but the first step in the Long March: "I thought I had made a great leap forward," she says, "but in fact I had only taken the first timid steps." And the film ends with the title: "End of a beginning."

The parallels with what actually happened in Nanterre and Paris in May 1968 are quite clear; almost terrifyingly prophetic is the long sequence-shot of Véronique and Communist writer Francis Jeanson on a train from Nanterre to Paris. Jeanson, in this scene, sets out almost word for word what was going to be the French Communist Party's attitude towards the May revolution.

The tone of the film is cool, as befits what is largely a conversation piece. Although the subject-matter is violence and revolution, the manner of the film is quasi-eighteenth century, rational, argued, methodical: *La Philosophie dans le Boudoir*, minus sex. Or almost. One scene seems significant of Godard's changing (or changed) view of love. In what purports simply to be Véronique's attempt to explain to Guillaume that in literature and art one can fight on two fronts simultaneously, she arranges a little practical demonstration. Guillaume has declared that he cannot understand how she can even listen to the gramophone and write at the same time, so she puts a bit of nineteenth-century romantic music on the machine and says: "I don't love you any more. I don't love your face, your eyes, your mouth; I don't love the colour of your sweaters any more. You bore me more than you can imagine. . . . You keep me from working, you fill me with anguish, you're too complicated. And I hate the way you talk about things without knowing what you're even talking about. I don't love you any more. Now do you understand?" Guillaume thinks he does, and is very sad. Then, in the proper eighteenth-century manner, she cheerfully rounds on him with: "Well, you see, one can very easily do two things at once, both music and language." "Right," says Guillaume, "but you had me scared for a while."

And indeed, he was right to be frightened, for it seems to me that the sense of this scene goes beyond its apparent purpose. It is one of the key scenes of recent Godard: this cold and calculated tone seems totally to have replaced the romanticism of the earlier films. The contrast between the romantic music on the gramophone and the dry cruelty of her words reinforces the contrast between what she says about Guillaume and the seemingly prosaic remark about his sweaters. It also points up graphically a certain generation gap both sentimental and political, and prepares us for the dehumanised world of *Weekend* and *One Plus One*. Behind the limpid eyes of Véronique lies the 'terrorism' of the cultural revolution, and what Godard takes to be the new face of Youth.

La Chinoise was labelled "A Film in the Making"; *Weekend* is termed "A Film Lost in the Cosmos" or, alternatively, "A Film Found on the Scrap-Heap". Actually, it is more classically constructed than *La Chinoise*, and for its first two-thirds, at least, the plot line is both clear and coherent. The film seems to have come out of that remark Godard made a few years ago about how contemporary French society closely resembled prostitution. People, he said, are prostituting themselves all week long, working

134

at jobs they don't like, selling things they don't believe in, and all for what? To be able to buy a car and spend the weekend at the sea. But all they find is blocked highways and traffic jams. He has taken this basic notion and turned the idea of a weekend on the road into an apocalyptic metaphor for contemporary society.

The film begins with a young middle-class couple setting out in their middle-class Dauphine in order to try to wheedle some money from mother, who lives deep in Normandy. Their departure is preceded by the wife's monumental monologue in which she unveils her sexual preoccupations, and, perhaps correspondingly, a mock-heroic scene which might be called "The Battle of the Scraped Fender", one of those ever-recurring scenes in French life today when The Car's mystical significance has to be protected against The Others, even with the aid of fire-arms, as in this case.

The usual weekend jam on the highways is evoked in a single brilliantly controlled shot which lasts for a full ten minutes. We track along stalled cars, bloodied victims of car crashes, the whole accompanied by a symphony of klaxons. As one of the punctuating titles puts it, "From the French Revolution to U.N.R. [the Gaullist party] weekends", i.e., two hundred years of so-called social progress to arrive at this travesty of a civilisation.

When, after an hour of the film, they arrive at his mother's house she refuses to give them any money. By this time all the veneer of civilisation has been stripped from them, so, in counterpoint to shots of a rabbit being skinned, they hack her down. As another title says: "Just a Tuesday during the Hundred Years War". And on the road, the wife has been raped by a tramp; "Du côté de chez Lewis Carroll" a milk-maid has been burned alive; two representatives of the Third World have mercilessly harangued us: in short, contemporary society has been revealed in all its horror.

On the way back to Paris, the couple's picnic is interrupted by a band of Maoist hippies who have taken over the Seine-et-Oise. From this point, the film takes off, leaving *Les Carabiniers* far behind, a model even of elegant civilisation. And the camp site of the hippies becomes a horrific parody of the joys of the

La Chinoise: "The first steps on the long march . . ." →

Politique et crime
A) l'impérialisme universitaire bourgeois

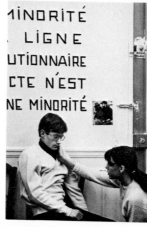

MINORITÉ
LIGNE
UTIONNAIRE
CTE N'EST
NE MINORITÉ

Weekend: "From the French Revolution . . . to the Chinese Apocalypse"

countryside, as they all sit down to a charcoal-broiled Englishman, a tourist who had unluckily happened that way. This idyll by the algae-covered pond is interrupted by a final shoot-up. "One cannot go beyond the horror of the bourgeoisie except by more horror still." But the Maoist hippies have at least made one convert: Mireille Darc, playing the depraved bourgeoise, finds here her Damascus road: "I'll go with you," she announces.

One of the master-strokes of the film was in fact the casting of Mireille Darc, that idol of French sex films, and Jean Yanne, who in his brilliant vulgarity could be said to represent the somewhat less than average Frenchman in this vicious satire of French life. So great had Godard's prestige become that the film was financed by a big company solely because Mlle Darc, with one film left to go in her contract, systematically refused all projects until she was offered what she wanted: Godard. And both her faith in him and his good sense in using her were vindicated. Dramatically, this was Godard's most hard-hitting, most fast-moving film in some time. Like *La Chinoise*, it was filmed in colour, but instead of the cool tones and white backgrounds of that film, *Weekend* is gory with the hardest yellows and reds imaginable.

If *Weekend* did for French society what *Made in U.S.A.* did for America, it is none the less true that *Weekend* was more conventionally constructed and written than *Made in U.S.A.* or *La Chinoise*. In some ways, even, it could be considered as a kind of bourgeois comedy which had somehow gone frighteningly off the rails. Godard's next film, *Le Gai Savoir*, marks a return to the dislocated form of *Made in U.S.A.* and *La Chinoise*. At the same time, it makes a 'great leap forward'. Of course, it is difficult from this point on to be absolutely certain of the chronology of Godard's films: certainly he began *Le Gai Savoir* in December 1967; on the other hand, it only came out in 1969, first at the Berlin Festival and then in London and at the New York Film Festival. It has still to be seen in France. Furthermore, there was a long gap between the shooting of the film and its final editing, so that it is impossible to say just how much of the film preceded the events of May 1968 and how much came after.

Weekend: "Travesty of a Civilisation" →

The film began as a project for French Television: an adaptation of Rousseau's classic work on education, *Emile*. The film Godard made turned out to be about language. Godard has always been both critic and film-maker, so there is nothing surprising in the fact that *Le Gai Savoir* is an essay, a pamphlet, even. There is, at last, no plot at all. A young couple (Jean-Pierre Léaud and Juliet Berto) sit in a television studio for an hour and a half, talking. Occasionally, shots of street scenes are intercut; otherwise, the film puritanically sticks to the two characters and their conversations about language.

The recently rediscovered writings of the German critic Walter Benjamin shed much light on the film, and indeed on Godard's recent development, not as a film-maker, but as a critic who uses film instead of paper. Benjamin's great unfinished work, *Paris, Capital of the Nineteenth Century*, was to have been a study of the complex links between economic evolution and cultural facts. Before his untimely death in 1940, Benjamin began to feel certain that this, in fact, was the critic's essential task. Like Godard, Benjamin was the victim of more and more frequent psychological depressions, and this—combined with the ever-growing Fascist threat of the late 1930s—brought his work to an ever more exacerbated state. Like the flame between two carbon arcs, he was stretched, almost to breaking point, between Marxist politics and the metaphysics of language: "The most worn-out Communist platitude," he wrote, "means more than the most profound bourgeois thought, because the latter has only one true meaning, that of *apology*, of class-justification."

Godard has always been as sensitive to cultural climates as the most intellectual barometer, so I doubt whether the comparison with Benjamin is fortuitous; equally important is the recent French vogue for linguistics and in particular for the new culture-hero, Noam Chomsky. From his leafings through Chomsky and the other linguistic philosophers, Godard seems to have reached the conclusion that language is the key to many of our problems. It is the enemy; as Juliet Berto says at the beginning of the film: "I want to learn, to teach myself, to teach everyone that we must turn

142

back against the enemy that weapon with which he attacks us: Language." "Yes," replies Léaud, "we have to start again from zero." "No, before we start again, we must first go *back* to zero."

Going back to zero of course implies a disintegration of man and his language. This ties in with Chomsky's statement that the renewal of the study of language ought to lead to a liberation from all our behaviouristic conditioning, and ultimately to a political criticism of our alienation. All thought has been, consciously or unconsciously, bound up with the conditioning of bourgeois society of the past hundred years. It takes great effort to look at everything afresh, to call everything, even words, into question; and in *Le Gai Savoir* Godard has attempted this most arduous of intellectual exercises.

There are moments when he seems to have taken his task too literally. When he breaks up the word 'cinema' on the soundtrack into a selection of phonemes (Cin/e/ma or C/i/n/e/ma), the result is less an illustration of the necessary disintegration of language than an annoying return to his semi-aphasiac anagrams. And the sequences in which the film is divested first of its soundtrack, and then of its visuals, do not seem to me to make any really valid contribution. The same is certainly true of that curious method of underlining single letters in a handwritten title which he developed in the Ciné-tracts. Sometimes the underlined letters spell out a word; at other times they simply form chains of 'u's, 'n's, 'i's and 'o's. Even if one does construe the word 'Union', does it really help? In either case, the technique—or tic—is less than illuminating. And his invention of the word 'Misotodiman' (a melange of method and sentiment) as a definition of images and sounds also fringes more on the aphasiac than on the heuristic.

One cannot, however, judge *Le Gai Savoir* as an ordinary film; it is meant to be not 'representation, but presentation', not a film, but an idea for the film of the future; in fact, it is left unfinished. She: "It's more or less nothingness that we have discovered, no?" He: "In other words, this film is a failure. And yet, no, not entirely. Not at all, even. Listen; what better ideal to propose to the men of today, one which would be above and beyond themselves,

Le Gai Savoir: Jean-Pierre Léaud, Juliet Berto →

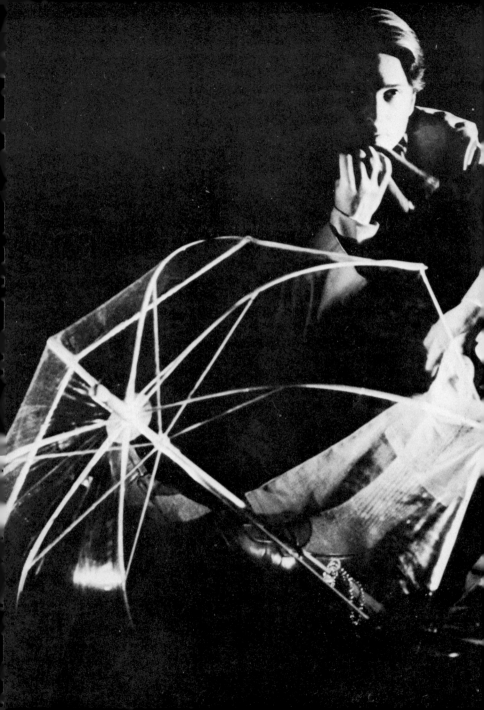

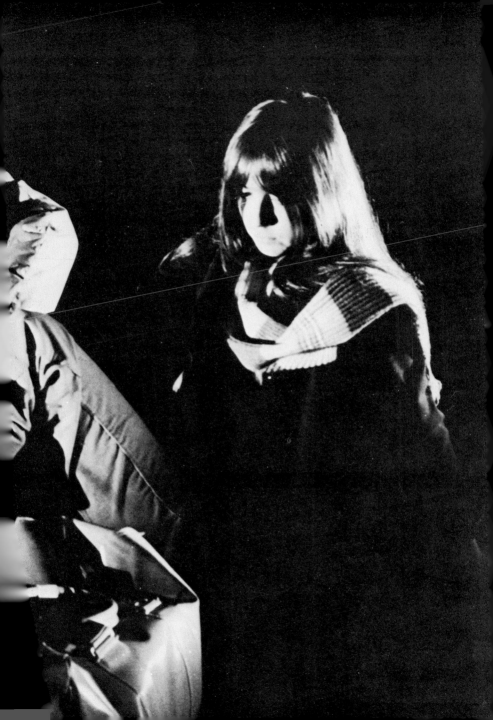

if not the reconquest, through knowledge, of the nothingness they themselves have discovered." So to Bertolucci is left the sequence of the girl's song, to Straub the analysis of the Family, and to Glauber Rocha that of the pillage of the Third World. *Le Gai Savoir* is only meant as an attempt to draw guide-lines; it only points the way towards the film of the future. At least, this is Godard's avowed intention. But how does it relate to his *own* future, how to his own past? There are, of course, elements in the film which resemble his earlier work. The first image, for example, of the orange-ribbed, transparent umbrella is as beautiful as anything he has ever done. The photography of Juliet Berto and Jean-Pierre Léaud is good enough for a shampoo commercial, so lustrously does it render their hair, shining with mysterious highlights. The Cuban revolutionary hymn with which Godard ends most of the episodes, the piano sonata which turns up as punctuation; the extraordinary mask effects, first with Léaud's face hidden behind hers, then the opposite, and finally, and most effectively, with her lips synch-ing his words spoken from behind her. There are remarkably effective camera movements going from left to right to pick up Léaud, then Mlle Berto, and then, in the same shot, further right mysteriously to catch Léaud again. Juliet Berto's yellow gown with its purple peignoir seen against the figures of comic-strip heroes, the neatly invisible construction of what looks to be a formless film.

But this kind of aesthetic approach would presumably run totally counter to Godard's intentions. He did not want to make an 'aesthetic object': the work of art is all too easily assimilated by the very society it is attacking. The work of art can be isolated, defused, reabsorbed by society: recuperated, to use the jargon.

Indeed, perhaps these 'beauties' I have catalogued were involuntary. Or more probably, they slipped through Godard's ideological guard. Certainly, in the two films that followed, *Un Film Comme les Autres* and *One Plus One*, there were fewer of these 'lapses'. And this raises the question: is Godard's systematic—almost religious—sacrifice of all his aesthetic trump cards entirely motivated by ideological reasons? Or rather, is it a kind of psychological despoiling, a masochistic denuding? I think the final answer will elude us for another few years, or at least until his two new films come out, *East Wind* and *British Sounds*. Meanwhile, on the basis of the films immediately following *Le Gai Savoir* (*One Plus One* and *Un Film Comme les Autres*), Godard does not seem yet to have found his way into the new stage of his development which *Le Gai Savoir* so bravely heralded. Whatever its faults, its occasional intellectual dishonesty, its paranoid moments, *Le Gai Savoir* somehow manages to hold together, to glow with that inner life of the eternal present, the sheer formal beauty of the momentarily resolved contradiction between abstraction and reality, between love and pain.

Un Film Comme les Autres seems to have been made some time during May and June of 1968. Legend has it that there is only one shot in the whole two-hour film, but this is not true. Nor is it true that the camera never moves; there are a few lateral pans now and then. Furthermore, there are a large number of newsreel cut-ins. Legend again has it that the whole film consists of views of tall grass, while on the soundtrack one can hear the discussion of the people hidden by the grass; again, this is not quite true, for we often see the bodies of the group, the man's polka-dot shirt, a girl's hair, her beautiful red and green peppermint-striped blouse, and once in a while we even see a face or two. This, reportedly, was pure accident. Legend again has it that Godard was not there during much of the shooting and so was unable to assure that none of the faces would be seen. The truth of this I have not been able to establish.

It is true that the film is made up of two one-hour-long 16-mm. reels, and one is meant to toss a coin to decide which reel comes first. On the other hand, there is a kind of end to the film: the Italian Communist song, "Bandiera Rossa", wells up on the soundtrack to signal the climax of the movie. Ultimately, it is a very boring film, though there are a few things here and there. Again, perhaps irrelevantly, some of the shots are extremely striking: the group half hidden by a clump of yellow flowers; the girl's blouse;

a shot of the girl seen from behind, with her long hair dangling down against the brown corduroy knee of one of the boys. Mostly, the discussion is on an extremely elementary level; much of it is repetitious. But then once in a while someone comes out with a relevant remark, like: "People, bourgeois people, often think that the worker's life is just like that of the bourgeois, only less comfortable, less good; but in fact, the worker's life is different from that of the bourgeois, and not just quantitatively." "There is," someone says, "no common language," and one feels that this is a problem that worries Godard. He is too honest to cheat, as it were, and yet he knows that his films, in the only way he can make them, are inaccessible to most workers. As he said to the Cubans, he only wants to make films that belong to *both* of them, i.e., to Jean-Luc Godard as well as to the Cubans. In his next film, *One Plus One*, there is the revealing line of dialogue: "There is only one way to be an intellectual revolutionary, and that is to give up being an intellectual."

In *One Plus One* he almost succeeds. "I want to make the film as simply as possible," he declared, "almost like an amateur film. What I want above all is to destroy the idea of culture. Culture is an alibi of imperialism. There is a Ministry of War. There is also a Ministry of Culture. Therefore, culture is war." One does not have to be an expert logician to find something wrong with this syllogism. And yet faulty logic can be artistically productive; in this case, I do not think it has been.

One Plus One began as a project by a novice Greek producer, Mrs Eleni Collard, for a film about abortion to be directed in England by Jean-Luc Godard. Then the abortion laws were changed, and the project took a new turn: Godard said he would make a film in England, providing the producers could get either the Beatles or the Rolling Stones. Mme Collard, now working with the Hon. Michael Pearson and actor Iain Quarrier, got the Rolling Stones and a budget of £180,000. And on 30 May 1968 Godard came to London to make the film. Godard's idea was to make a film on two parallel themes: construction (the Stones

recording—and making—a song) and destruction (the suicide of a white girl, to be played by Mlle Wiazemsky, when deserted by her black boyfriend in favour of a Black Power guerrilla band).

This plan was soon abandoned, and now the film has no narrative at all. It begins by presenting us with a Bolivian revolutionary hiding in a London lavatory "before waiting on the beach for Uncle Mao's yellow submarine to come and get me." To while away the time, he reads from a political/pornographic novel. This is interspersed with long takes of the Stones rehearsing a new song ("Sympathy for the Devil"); shots of a group of Black Power militants in a junkyard by the Thames; a television interview with Eve Democracy (Anne Wiazemsky) in a cool green forest—she only answers "Yes" and "No" to a series of questions about the relationship of culture and revolution; sequences in a pornographic bookshop where producer Iain Quarrier reads aloud extracts from *Mein Kampf*. All these sequences are equally intercut by shortish scenes in which Mlle Wiazemsky rushes about London writing protest slogans on every available surface.

The title of the film is important. As Godard said when the producers insisted on dubbing, over the last reel, the *completed* version of "Sympathy for the Devil"—"'One Plus One' does not mean 'one plus one equals two'. It just means what it says, 'one plus one'." So we are obliged to take it as it stands; a series of fragmentary fragments, and it is presumably for us to edit the film. This accords very well with recent theories of aleatory art; unfortunately, I doubt that, even had one the opportunity to edit the film, it would add up to much. But now I've fallen into Godard's trap: it is not meant to add up, and it won't. This would not matter so much, were not the individual elements so almost entirely lifeless. This may in part be due to the fact that the text is in English. One knew how important the soundtrack was to Godard's films, but *One Plus One* proves it is primordial. The same phenomenon can be observed in the English songs of the late Edith Piaf. One had thought her great talent was the quality of her voice, its emotional muscularity. But it turns out, on the evidence of her English-language renditions, to have been as much, if not more, in her handling of the words, the French words. And so perhaps the English language is partly responsible for the paleness of *One Plus One*.

The defenders of the film claim that it cannot be regarded as an aesthetic object: it is simply a report, or rather a terrifying comic strip, the meaning of which, the code, has been lost. This film is in fact the zero to which Godard said in *Le Gai Savoir* that we must return. But it is possible to think that the film is less a consciously chosen attempt to reach absolute zero than the result of a certain degree of disorder in Godard caused by the circumstances of the making of the film. He did not ever want to make a film in England, and being obliged to leave Paris in the middle of the May revolution undoubtedly caused a degree of strain. During shooting, Brian Jones was arrested, as earlier was Terence Stamp who was due to play the Quarrier role. The roof of the Stones' recording studio caught fire, and as a result Godard went back to France. He later returned, only to have the shooting of the Black Power sequences jinxed by rain. He left for Paris again, came back. . . . So when at the end of the film one hears a voice suspiciously like Godard's saying that he is fed up and wants to go home, one might conclude that this was an ill-starred project from beginning to end, and let it go at that.

But other films have survived more disastrous events during the shooting. It seems to me that Godard is uniquely unfitted to make the kind of film he thinks he *ought* to be making. One can imagine another director (although, who?) succeeding, but not Godard. He can get along without a story (as witness *Le Gai Savoir*), but it would seem he cannot do without the lyricism which recently he has been trying so hard to suppress. And that is perhaps why the scenes of Eve Democracy in her green shade, or the lyricism of the Stones in their rehearsal periods, are the only sequences that come alive in *One Plus One*. Godard has said that: "What is alive is not what's on the screen but what is between the audience and the screen." True, perhaps, but in order for something to come alive between audience and screen there must first be something alive between the director (who is, after all, the first member of a film's audience) and what is on the screen. And with the exceptions noted above, there seems to be very little that is alive between director and screen in this film. Perhaps the corollary to "There is only one way to be an intellectual revolutionary, and that is to give up being an intellectual" is that, *for Godard at least*, there is only one way to become a revolutionary film-maker—and that is to give up being a film-maker.

Now, at the end of 1969, Godard seems to be at a crossroads. After *One Plus One*, he began a film for Leacock-Pennebaker. Called variously *One American Movie*, or *1 A.M.*, it is still unfinished. After shooting roughly ninety per cent of the film Godard went back to France. He later announced that he was abandoning the film; then in September 1969 that he would after all return to the States to finish it. He has not yet. In Rome, accompanied by Daniel Cohn-Bendit and thirty student advisers, he shot *Vento dell'est* in the summer of 1969. The film was supposed to be ready by November, but he is apparently still editing it. He did complete a film for British television called *British Sounds*; I have not seen it, but the few who have (it has not yet appeared on television) say it is a remarkable agit-prop film.

Godard's future development is impossible to predict. We shall have to wait for *East Wind*, for *British Sounds*, for *One American Movie*. But most of all, for the films he has not even begun to make. . . .

One Plus One: Black Power in Battersea; Eve Democracy and The Serpent; Sympathy for the Devil

Appendix: Shorts and Sketches

Apart from his prolific output of feature films, Godard has made a number of shorts and episodes for sketch films. These are interesting not only in themselves, but also either because they shed light on his features or because they were in fact preliminary sketches for them. Many have not been seen widely, if at all, in England or America, so it seems worthwhile to run through them chronologically.

Godard's very first short was *Opération Béton*, which he shot in 35 mm on the site of a dam in Switzerland (La Grande Dixence) and financed with the money he earned as a construction worker on the dam. He was twenty-four years old at the time, and what is so extraordinary about the film is that it is so very ordinary. Cleanly photographed and efficiently made, it hardly differs in any significant way from the 'class' short film production of the period, with its literate commentary and classical score. It was distributed in France paired with, of all things, *Tea and Sympathy*.

His second short, *Une Femme Coquette*, however, is extremely rewarding. In a sense, all of Godard is already there, but naturally in a rather crude form. It is based on that Maupassant story *Le Signe* which was later to serve as the germ of the so-called 'Swedish' episode in *Masculin Féminin*: the film-within-the-film. The plot is about a respectable young married woman who, fascinated by the come-on look with which a prostitute attracts her customers, is tempted to try it out. Just to see if it works; and it does. Pursued by a stranger to the very door of her apartment, she finally gives in to him because she is expecting her husband at any moment, and this

Masculin Féminin: the "Swedish sequence" based on the
Maupassant story *Le Signe* (Eva Britt Strandberg, Birger
Malmsten)

seems the quickest way of getting the man out of the house. It is
curious that although the short follows the story closely, it stops at
the moment the importunate stranger forces his way into the
apartment; and it is precisely what happens afterwards that forms
the subject of the *Masculin Féminin* episode.

Stylistically, many of Godard's devices are already in evidence.
'Rapid' cutting, unmatched shots, and hand-held camera; pleonas-
tic use of dialogue (we see the words of a letter, while the actress
simultaneously reads them aloud); flash-shots; the big American
car; false timing (as the narrator says she saw a man leave the
prostitute's flat, we actually see him *entering* it); alternation of
sunny takes with grey ones in what are supposed to be two immediately consecutive shots. For the first time, too, we see one of his
actresses shaking her head, fluffing up her hair, swirling it around.
Finally, Godard himself makes an appearance in the film as one of
the prostitute's customers.

The film is fascinating now, but one wonders what one's
reactions would have been at the time it was made. Pretty negative,
I suppose, because one could not have been sure that Godard was,
so to speak, doing it all on *purpose*, or whether he just didn't know
any better.

His next two shorts, *Tous les Garçons s'appellent Patrick* and *Charlotte et son Jules*, were more polished, perhaps because they were also less ambitious. In *Une Femme Coquette* Godard seems to have been trying out all his cinematic ideas at once, as often happens in a first or second film. In the next two shorts, he is already more disciplined, more restrained: this makes them better, but less exciting. *Tous les Garçons s'appellent Patrick* has a scenario by Eric Rohmer, and in fact it is very much like one of his *Contes Moraux*. Charlotte meets Patrick who tries to pick her up. She leaves; he then meets Véronique and flirts with her. But the two girls are room-mates, and that evening they talk about the two attractive men they have met. The next day, seeing him flirting with yet another girl, they discover it was the same man. The setting is the Luxembourg Gardens and its surrounding student cafés. For the first time Godard uses newspapers and magazines: in the café a man sits next to the girls reading the weekly *Arts*: the headline is "The French cinema is dying under the weight of false legends."

Charlotte et son Jules was scripted by Godard, and, in fact, although the lead is played by Jean-Paul Belmondo, it is Godard's voice we hear (Belmondo had to go to do his military service). The story is pure shaggy dog: Charlotte comes back to see her ex-lover; he imagines she has changed her mind and come back for good. After a long monologue in which he alternately scolds and coaxes her, he discovers that she has only returned to collect her toothbrush. The monologue is already pure Godard in style: "Behind a woman's face, one sees her soul" and "Je t'aime; non, je ne t'aime plus; si, je t'aime." In spite of its comic frame, the story ends in near-tragedy: when Charlotte leaves, Belmondo puts his hands up to his face in a kind of Pierrot gesture, and we realise with a shock that all has not been as funny as it seemed.

The genesis of his last short, *Une Histoire d'Eau*, was very strange. It began with François Truffaut, so let him tell the story:

"I was always fascinated by floods; I liked seeing them in newsreels except that I always said to myself, what a shame there are never any actors in such sequences. When one winter there were some floods in the Paris area, I went to Pierre Braunberger, the producer, and said, 'I can get Jean-Claude Brialy and a girl; give me a little raw stock, and we'll improvise a film.' He gave it to us, and off we went. But by that time, there wasn't much flood-water left, and besides, when we did find some flooded areas, we didn't have the heart to shoot any film. It wasn't, after all, so very funny, and we were ashamed to be making a comic film with all those homeless people. Still, we did shoot the 2,400 feet of film we had, and went back to Paris. I thought we had made a mistake, so I asked Braunberger to let us abandon the whole idea. In the meantime, Godard had seen the rushes, and he said he would like to try to do something with the material, as long as he could ignore our original conception. He worked very quickly to keep the costs down, writing the commentary, and choosing the music. When I saw the finished product, I thought it was very entertaining, but I didn't want my name on the credits because I had had so little to do with it. Finally, we agreed to co-sign it."

I don't find the result as amusing as all that, but it is significant in its revelation of Godard's attitude towards filmed reality as something to be played with, re-created, re-formed by the process of editing. Further, it displays his interest in the kind of commentary that doesn't actually comment on what we are seeing, but acts rather in counterpoint to it. The music he chose is a *mélange* of eighteenth-century Rococo, jazz, and some *put-put-put* drums which appropriately gives the feeling both of motor-boats and pumping machines. This time, it is Brialy who is dubbed by Godard. Why, I don't know; perhaps just to save time.

Godard's first sketch came three years later in 1961, when Franco-London remade *Les Sept Péchés Capitaux*. Godard chose, or was assigned, "Sloth", and he made a tiny masterpiece of it. The basic joke is that the hero is so lazy that even when he is seduced by a charming girl, he finally rejects her when the time

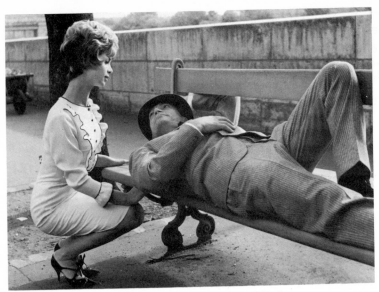

"La Paresse": episode from *Les Sept Péchés Capitaux* (Nicole Mirel and Eddie Constantine)

comes to go to bed, because it will be too much trouble to get dressed again afterwards. Eddie Constantine plays the lead because, said Godard, "I wanted to use a famous actor who was well known as a personality. I could do it with Constantine because he's a solid block, a block of intelligence and precision, but a block just the same." Part of the joke, of course, was to have an actor who is well known for his intrepid exploits playing a man who is too lazy to tie his own shoes, but the choice seems also to have been dictated by Godard's penchant for documentary.

The episode all takes place during a journey from the film studios at Saint-Cloud along the Seine to the girl's flat in Paris; here, for the first time, I think, we have an example of Godard's unrealistic use of sound. Throughout the first half of the sketch, one hears what one takes to be the car radio playing lazy Hawaiian music; when the car goes through an underpass, the music stops. But then, in the flat, it quite surprisingly begins again. This sequence also contains one of Godard's most fascinating cuts on movement. The camera, placed in the car, moves along the boulevard, down into an underpass, starts up the ramp; then we cut to an ascending lift, from under which we see Constantine and the girl (who have presumably just emerged from it) making their way along the landing. Throughout the film, Constantine's laziness is contrasted with a continual change of shot: when they stop at a filling-station, the sequence is shot from many different angles while all the time Constantine is trying unsuccessfully to bribe the attendant to tie his shoe for him! (Godard originally wanted to use the heaviest— and presumably therefore, the 'laziest'—camera he could find, a Mitchell, but finally had to settle for an ordinary Debrie.)

The next sketch, "Le Nouveau Monde", was made for an Italian film first called *RoGoPaG* (the episodes were directed by Rossellini, Godard, Pasolini, and Gregoretti) and then, after it ran into trouble with the Italian censors because of the Pasolini sequence, *Let's Wash our Brains*.

"I'm going to make a sketch," said Godard, "about a man who goes out into the street; everything seems normal, but two or three little details reveal to him that everyone—including his fiancée— no longer thinks or reasons normally. He discovers, for example, that cafés are not called 'cafés' any more. And when his fiancée stands him up, it is not because she is no longer in love with him, but because she just thinks about time in a different way: they don't share the same logic. One day he sees in a newspaper that there has been an atomic explosion somewhere, and he says to himself that he must be the only man left on earth who has escaped its effects, who still thinks normally. Everything is the same, and yet different. What has happened is that all notion of cause and effect has disappeared." This is presented by Godard as a metaphorical illustration of an actual statement by the physicist Werner Heisenberg, which posits the disappearance of the cause and effect relationship in the new world of atomic physics.

"Le Nouveau Monde" is a kind of first sketch for *Alphaville*, and it bears many resemblances to it. The predatory girls in

"Le Nouveau Monde": episode from *RoGoPaG*. The swimming pool (Alexandra Stewart) and the Champs-Elysées (Godard and Jean-Marc Bory)

Alphaville who use their knives to finish off the victims executed in a swimming-pool are foreshadowed here by the girls who all have a knife strapped to their thighs, a phenomenon the hero notices first in a swimming-pool sequence. But most important of all, this anticipation of the future is shot in the Paris of today, just as *Alphaville* will be. Here, Godard doesn't have quite enough confidence in the device to carry it off completely, so he introduces shots of the Eiffel Tower cut off halfway up and the Arc de Triomphe sliced horizontally in two. Nevertheless, the basic idea is there, and its effect is already very disturbing.

Le Grand Escroc was supposed to form part of an episode film called *Les Plus Belles Escroqueries du Monde*, but for reasons which have never been fully explained, it was not released with it. Instead, a few years later, it accompanied a revival of King Vidor's *Our Daily Bread* at several Paris art houses. *Le Grand Escroc* is the French title of Herman Melville's *The Confidence Man*, and the heroine of the film is called Patricia Leacock: Patricia, because she is played by Jean Seberg, and that was her name in *A Bout de Souffle*; Leacock, because she too is a roving television reporter. The setting is Marrakesh, and the confidence man is a strange Arab (played by Charles Denner) who goes round the Medina distributing money to the poor—but the bills are counterfeit. Patricia finally tracks him down, and persuades him to let her film him: "I make *cinéma vérité*: truth motion pictures, like Monsieur Rouch," she explains. "My programme is called 'The Most Extraordinary Man I Ever Met'; it's sponsored by the *Reader's Digest*." When she reproaches him, in the course of her filming, with cheating poor people by giving them fake money, he replies that since she is making a film about him in order to sell it to other people, she is therefore no better than he.

The implication, of course, is that *cinéma vérité* does not give us the truth. It, too, is a kind of counterfeit passed off as the real thing: like the incident Patricia reports of a friend who bought some photographs of Karl Marx from the Polish government, sketched on a different beard, and then sold them to pious peasants as portraits of Christ. Or like Godard's view of Richard Leacock:

"Le Grand Escroc": episode from *Les Plus Belles Escroqueries du Monde* which was, however, never shown with it.
Jean Seberg reading Herman Melville's *The Confidence Man*

"There's no point in having sharp images if you've got fuzzy ideas.
Leacock's lack of subjectivity leads him ultimately to a lack of
objectivity. He doesn't even know that he is a *metteur en scène*, that
pure reportage doesn't exist."

"Montparnasse-Levallois": episode from *Paris vu par . . .*
(Philippe Hiquilly and Johanna Shimkus)

Paradoxically enough, Godard's next sketch was to be filmed by a well-known *cinéma vérité* cameraman, Albert Maysles. "Montparnasse-Levallois" is a slightly altered version of the story told by Belmondo in *Une Femme est une Femme*, and forms part of a film called *Paris vu par . . .* which contains six episodes, each set in a different quarter of Paris. All the sketches were filmed in sixteen millimetre colour and then successfully blown up to thirty-five millimetre.

The story concerns a feather-brained girl who sends two letters to her two boy-friends; after posting them she thinks she has mixed up the envelopes. She rushes to tell each of them in turn not to pay any attention to the note, only to find that she has *not* made a mistake. By this time, it is too late: she has revealed to both men her double-dealing, and she is ditched by both. The main difference between story and sketch is that Godard has added a questionable gimmick: one of the men is a metal-worker in a garage, and the other an abstract sculptor in iron whose atelier looks almost exactly like the garage.

Many people have felt that the episode was more Maysles than Godard, and there is some reason to think that this is true. Godard has said, "We shot the film in three or four takes, and then we cut them into pieces." Others have suggested that Godard was not able himself to be present during much of the shooting. In any case, "Montparnasse-Levallois" is only very mildly amusing; it is curious, however, that Godard or somebody has managed to turn Johanna Shimkus, the heroine, into yet another (after Brigitte Bardot and Macha Méril) version of Anna Karina. It should also be noted that the sculptor is played by a rather well-known artist, and that his own atelier is used.

Godard's subsequent sketch is called "L'An 2,000" or "Anticipation" and is part of *Le Plus Vieux Métier du Monde* (subtitle, *L'Amour à Travers les Ages*). It deals with prostitution in the future, a reasonably commercial subject. The producer, however, was a little worried, and before Godard began the film, he said to him, "Listen, Monsieur Godard, it's going to be all right, isn't it? I mean, it's going to be exciting?" "Well, it all depends what you mean," replied Godard teasingly; "I find *Gertrude* very exciting." "Well, I mean, there's going to be some action, isn't there?" "Oh," said Godard, "I don't know; I might make it all in freeze-frames." Whereupon the producer, scandalised, replied, "Oh, Monsieur Godard, you wouldn't do that to me, would you? You, such an *honest* young man!"

Actually, he didn't use many freeze-frames, and the sketch is what you might call action-packed—for Godard, that is. But there still was trouble not with the producer, but with the exhibitors. Godard's sketch was photographed with a kind of monochrome 'bleached-out' effect. Every so often, the one colour changes from red to yellow to blue and back again, and a narrator announces each of these changes with the words "Couleur Européenne", or "Couleur Soviétique", or "Couleur Chinoise". Unfortunately, the film was first released in an all-yellow version (shades of *La*

"L'An 2,000": episode from *Le Plus Vieux Métier du Monde*
(Jean-Pierre Léaud, Jacques Charrier, Marilù Tolo)

Chinoise!) apparently because the exhibitors found the bleaching-out Avedon-like effects too hard to 'read' and the changes of colour distracting. Quite illogically, however, they left the announcements of the colour changes on the soundtrack.

The subject of the sketch somewhat resembles *Alphaville*: a member of the Sovietoamerican Army from another galaxy arrives at the Technical Capital of Earth (actually, Orly Airport). The immigration control (they examine each passenger's palm) discovers, one imagines, that he is sexually deprived, and so he is sent to the adjoining hotel (actually the Hilton-Orly) to receive 'treatment'. The first prostitute who arrives does not, however, excite him, largely because she never says a word. A second is sent for: she (Anna Karina) arrives dressed in a long white crinoline, and announces that she is "Sentimental Love"—the first girl was "Physical Love". "Integral Specialisation" has proceeded so far that one kind of prostitute is specialised in the act of love, another in the language of love. The latter never undresses or touches her partner; she just talks.

However, our intrepid intergalactic visitor teaches Miss Sentimental Love that there *is* one part of the body that can both speak and make love: the mouth. They kiss, and for the first time the image is seen in full colour.

Godard maintained that the colour effects were the whole point of the film and that without them it could not be judged. This of course was so, but even in monochrome there are some extremely beautiful effects, particularly in his use of the banked landing-lights of the airfield, which came out looking very much like something from another planet.

Fortunately, however, Godard subsequently prevailed upon the producers of the film, and the episode in its original form was shown first at the Trieste Science Fiction Festival, and then at an art house in Paris as part of a programme called 'Star Short Films'. Seeing it in its proper form bore out the importance of the various effects: the bleaching-out, the use of negative, and the constantly changing monochrome-red, yellow, blue, green. To be sure, it *is* a little hard to read, but it more than makes up for this in heightened meaning and visual interest.

At about the same time that Godard was making *La Chinoise*, he contributed an episode to *Loin du Viêt-Nam*. This was a collective work, with contributions from Resnais, William Klein, Joris Ivens, Claude Lelouch and others, but it seems that the organising spirit was Chris Marker (who has listed himself only as one of the 'Principal Collaborators'). The purpose of the film was clearly didactic: each collaborator was, in his own way, to express his feelings and views on the Vietnam war. There are rumours that the Godard contribution, as it is now in the film, was his second try, the first having been rejected by the committee of collaborators. In any case, his 'episode', as it now stands, is the simplest of them all, and perhaps the most moving.

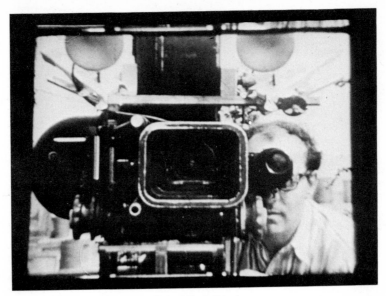

Loin du Viêt-Nam: Godard and the Mitchell

The episode consists of a monologue by Godard. Half-hidden behind an enormous Mitchell camera, one eye to the sight, he tells us that he had tried to go to North Vietnam a few years before, and that his application had been rejected: it appears that he seemed too frivolous or politically too unorthodox for the North Vietnamese. When that happened, he tells us, he decided that he would get some mention of the war into all of his succeeding films, whether it fitted or not. And I think one can say that he kept this promise.

Here, where the film's only point is precisely the war in Vietnam, he allows himself to speak directly. But what is most significant about the episode, at least in the light of his later development, is the very simplicity of his approach: he may physically be hidden behind the camera, but he is speaking directly to the *real* camera, as baldly as Jean-Pierre Léaud and Juliet Berto will do in *Le Gai Savoir.*

L'Aller Retour des Enfants Prodigues: The Witnesses

It would seem that this was the turning-point of his recent development: fiction is completely jettisoned in favour of direct speech.

Godard's most recent sketch is *L'Aller Retour des Enfants Prodigues*, or, as it was first called, *L'Enfant Prodigue*. It was made in 1967, to be part of a film called *Gospel '70* which was to have episodes by Lizzani (who produced the film), Bertolucci, Pasolini, Zurlini, and Godard. Godard's sketch was finished on time in 1967, but then the Zurlini episode became too long and was eventually released as a feature film (*Seduto alla sua Destra*) on its own. Meanwhile, the other episodes, all on Biblical themes, had been finished, but now one more was needed. Marco Bellocchio and Elda Tattoli were induced to contribute the final episode, but as Bellocchio announced he would have nothing to do with anything called *Gospel '70*, or indeed *Gospel* anything, the title of the film was changed to *Amore e Rabbia* (*Love and Rage*), and as such it was shown at the Berlin Festival of 1969. And indeed, the Bellocchio episode was very lay.

The plot of Godard's episode is a Titus and Berenice story of a French bourgeois girl and a proletarian man from the Third World who are forced to separate, each to follow his own destiny. The film is in both French and Italian (Nino Castelnuovo speaks Italian, and Christine Guého, French). The two main characters are 'doubled' by two observers (one French, Catherine Jourdan; one Italian, Paolo Pozzesi): they are witnesses, commentators and translators, for the film is so devised that everything of importance is spoken, one way or another, in both languages.

Shot on a shoestring, the episode is set entirely on a roof-garden in Paris, and it is very much a transitional work. There is still a good deal of the earlier Godard in the way it is filmed, but it also points clearly towards the later, more didactic style. But the curse on *Vangelo '70* still seems to persist; apart from the screening at the Berlin Festival and a few showings in Italy, *Love and Rage* has still to be seen widely.

To this catalogue of Godard's sketches and shorts must be added the *Ciné-Tracts*. As a direct result of the events of May, 1968, many French film-makers, perhaps led by Godard, made a series of three-minute film tracts. They are all silent, and mostly consist of a montage of still photographs with graphic inter-cuts. They are all on 16 mm. and are all anonymous (there are no credits), partly because of the need for discretion, and partly because the works were meant to be not individual expressions, but *oeuvres de combat*. Godard's handwriting is unmistakable in many of these tracts, but of course there is no way of being sure that he was therefore responsible for all the films that bear his distinctive calligraphy, although one can be reasonably sure that those which rely on the Godard trick (or tic) of underlining letters and syllables must be by him. After all, who else would think of extrapolating the word 'anal' from the word 'analyse'!

In France the *ciné-tracts* were shown only on an 'underground circuit'; abroad they were shown more openly, at the Venice and New York Film Festivals and at the National Film Theatre, for

Anne Wiazemsky in New York: Observing *1 A.M.* (photograph by Kate Taylor)

example. Given the form of the tracts, it was interesting to note the influence of Marker and Resnais, and the whole book-layout aspect of what has been called the 'Left Bank' group. It is also significant, and perhaps unfortunate, that some of the more annoying aspects of the tracts one ascribes to Godard can be found in his later films, like *Le Gai Savoir,* where the acrostic/aphasiac manner reaches new—and perhaps irrelevant—heights.

Filmography

Jean-Luc Godard

Born Paris, 3 December 1930

Studied at Nyon (Switzerland), the Lycée Buffon (Paris), and the Sorbonne (Certificat d'Ethnologie, 1949)

Published first articles on the cinema in *Gazette du Cinéma*, 1950

Travelled in North and South America, 1951

Wrote for *Cahiers du Cinéma* under the pseudonym of Hans Lucas, 1952

Worked on a dam construction site in Switzerland, where he shot his first film, *Opération Béton*, 1954

Wrote film reviews for *Arts*, 1956

Collaborated regularly on *Cahiers du Cinéma*, 1956–1959

Godard can be glimpsed briefly as an actor in *Une Femme Coquette, A Bout de Souffle, Le Petit Soldat, RoGoPaG, Le Mépris*. He has appeared, generally in small, non-speaking parts, in a number of other films: *Quadrille* (Jacques Rivette, 1950), *Présentation, ou Charlotte et son Steack* (Eric Rohmer, 1951), *Le Coup du Berger* (Jacques Rivette, 1956), *Paris Nous Appartient* (Jacques Rivette, 1958), *Le Signe du Lion* (Eric Rohmer, 1959), *Cléo de 5 à 7* (Agnès Varda, 1961), *Le Soleil dans l'Oeil* (Jacques Bourdon, 1961), *Shéhérazade* (Pierre Gaspard-Huit, 1962), *L'Espion* (Raoul Lévy, 1966).

Features

A Bout de Souffle (1959)

Production Company	Georges de Beauregard/Société Nouvelle de Cinéma (Paris)
Producer	Georges de Beauregard
Director	Jean-Luc Godard
Assistant Director	Pierre Rissient
Script	Jean-Luc Godard. Based on an idea by François Truffaut
Director of Photography	Raoul Coutard
Camera Operator	Claude Beausoleil
Editor	Cécile Decugis, Lila Herman
Artistic Supervisor	Claude Chabrol
Music	Martial Solal
Sound	Jacques Maumont

Jean-Paul Belmondo (*Michel Poiccard* alias *Laszlo Kovacs*), Jean Seberg (*Patricia Franchini*), Daniel Boulanger (*Police Inspector*), Jean-Pierre Melville (*Parvulesco*), Liliane Robin (*Minouche*), Henri-Jacques Huet (*Antonio Berrutti*), Van Doude (*The Journalist*), Claude Mansard (*Claudius Mansard*), Michel Fabre (*Plain-clothes Policeman*), Jean-Luc Godard (*An Informer*), Jean Domarchi (*A Drunk*), Richard Balducci (*Tolmatchoff*), Roger Hanin (*Carl Zombach*), Jean-Louis Richard (*A Journalist*), André-S. Labarthe, Jacques Siclier, Michel Mourlet, Jean Douchet, Philippe de Broca, Guido Orlando, Jacques Serguine, Louiguy, Virginie Ullmann, Emile Villion, José Bénazéraf, Madame Paul, Raymond Ravanbaz.

Filmed on location in Paris and Marseille, August–September 1959.

First shown in Paris, 16 March 1960; U.S.A., May 1961; G.B., July 1961. Running time, 90 mins.

Distributors: Impéria Films (France), BLC/British Lion (G.B.), Films-Around-the-World (U.S.A.).

U.S./G.B. title: BREATHLESS.

Le Petit Soldat (1960)

Production Company	Georges de Beauregard/Société Nouvelle de Cinéma (Paris)
Producer	Georges de Beauregard
Director	Jean-Luc Godard
Assistant Director	Francis Cognany
Script	Jean-Luc Godard
Director of Photography	Raoul Coutard
Camera Operator	Michel Latouche
Editor	Agnès Guillemot, Nadine Marquand, Lila Herman
Music	Maurice Leroux
Sound	Jacques Maumont

Michel Subor (*Bruno Forestier*), Anna Karina (*Véronica Dreyer*), Henri-Jacques Huet (*Jacques*), Paul Beauvais (*Paul*), Laszlo Szabo (*Laszlo*), Georges de Beauregard (*Activist Leader*), Jean-Luc Godard (*Bystander at railway station*), Gilbert Edard.

Filmed on location in Geneva, April–May 1960. Banned by the French Censor Board and Minister of Information; passed with minor cuts and first shown in Paris, 25 January 1963; G.B., June 1963; U.S.A. (at New York Film Festival, September 1965). Running time, 88 mins. Distributors: Impéria Films (France), Academy/Connoisseur (G.B.). G.B. title: THE LITTLE SOLDIER.

Une Femme est une Femme (1961)

Production Company	Rome-Paris Films (Paris)
Producer	Georges de Beauregard, Carlo Ponti
Production Manager	Philippe Dussart
Director	Jean-Luc Godard
Assistant Director	Francis Cognany
Script	Jean-Luc Godard. Based on an idea by Geneviève Cluny
Director of Photography	Raoul Coutard (Techniscope)
Colour Process	Eastman Colour
Editor	Agnès Guillemot, Lila Herman
Art Director	Bernard Evein
Music	Michel Legrand
Song "Chanson d'Angéla"	Michel Legrand, Jean-Luc Godard
Sound	Guy Villette

Jean-Paul Belmondo (*Alfred Lubitsch*), Anna Karina (*Angéla*), Jean-Claude Brialy (*Emile Récamier*), Marie Dubois (*Suzanne*), Nicole Paquin (*1st Prostitute*), Marion Sarraut (*2nd Prostitute*), Jeanne Moreau (*Woman in bar*), Catherine Demongeot.

Filmed in the Studio Saint-Maurice and on location in Paris, November 1960–January 1961. First shown at the Berlin Festival, 1 July 1961; Paris, 6 September 1961; U.S.A., November 1964 (previously at New York Film Festival, September 1964); G.B., March 1967 (previously at London Film Festival, October 1961). Running time, 84 mins.
Distributors: Unidex (France), Amanda (G.B.), Pathé Contemporary (U.S.A.).
U.S./G.B. title: A WOMAN IS A WOMAN.

Vivre sa Vie (1962)

Production Company	Films de la Pléiade (Paris)
Producer	Pierre Braunberger
Production Manager	Roger Fleytoux
Director	Jean-Luc Godard
Assistant Director	Bernard Toublanc-Michel, Jean-Paul Savignac
Script	Jean-Luc Godard. Documentation from *Où en est la prostitution?* by Marcel Sacotte
Director of Photography	Raoul Coutard
Camera Operator	Claude Beausoleil, Charles Bitsch
Editor	Agnès Guillemot, Lila Lakshmanan
Music	Michel Legrand
Song "Ma môme, elle joue pas les starlettes"	Jean Ferrat, Pierre Frachet
Sound	Guy Villette, Jacques Maumont

Anna Karina (*Nana Kleinfrankenheim*), Sady Rebbot (*Raoul*), André-S. Labarthe (*Paul*), Guylaine Schlumberger (*Yvette*), Brice Parain (*The Philosopher*), Peter Kassowitz [voice dubbed by Jean-Luc Godard] (*Young Man*), Dimitri Dinoff (*Dimitri*), Monique Messine (*Elizabeth*), Gérard Hoffmann (*Man to whom Nana is sold*), Gilles Quéant (*Client*), Paul Pavel (*The Photographer*), Eric Schlumberger (*Luigi*), Marcel Charton (*Policeman at typewriter*), Laszlo Szabo (*Wounded man who enters bar*), Gisèle Hauchecorne (*Concierge*), Odile Geoffroy (*Barmaid*), Jacques Florency (*Man in cinema*), Jean Ferrat (*Man at juke box who watches Nana*), Henri Atal (*Arthur*), Jean-Paul Savignac (*Young Soldier in bar*), Mario Botti (*The Italian*).

Filmed on location in Paris, February–March 1962. First shown at the Venice Film Festival, 28 August 1962; Paris, 20 September 1962; G.B., December 1962 (previously at London Film Festival, October 1962); U.S.A., September 1963. Running time, 85 mins. (cut by British censor to 82 mins.).
Distributors: Panthéon, Films de la Pléiade (France), Miracle (G.B.), Pathé Contemporary (U.S.A.).
U.S. title: MY LIFE TO LIVE; G.B. title: IT'S MY LIFE.

Les Carabiniers (1963)

Production Company	Rome-Paris Films (Paris)/Laetitia (Rome)
Producer	Georges de Beauregard, Carlo Ponti
Director	Jean-Luc Godard
Assistant Director	Charles Bitsch, Jean-Paul Savignac
Script	Jean-Luc Godard, Jean Gruault, Roberto Rossellini. Based on the play *I Carabinieri* by Benjamino Joppolo, adapted into French by Jacques Audiberti
Director of Photography	Raoul Coutard
Camera Operator	Claude Beausoleil
Editor	Agnès Guillemot, Lila Lakshmanan
Art Director	Jean-Jacques Fabre
Music	Philippe Arthuys
Sound	Jacques Maumont, Hortion

Marino Masè (*Ulysse*), Albert Juross (*Michel-Ange*), Geneviève Galéa (*Vénus*), Catherine Ribéro (*Cléopâtre*), Gérard Poirot (*1st Carabinier*), Jean Brassat (*2nd Carabinier*), Alvaro Gheri (*3rd Carabinier*), Barbet Schroeder (*Car Salesman*), Odile Geoffroy (*Young Communist Girl*), Roger Coggio and Pascale Audret (*The Couple in the car*), Catherine Durante (*Heroine of film-within-film*), Jean Gruault ("*Bébé's*" *Father*), Jean-Louis Comolli (*Soldier with the fish*), Wladimir Faters (*Revolutionary*), Jean Monsigny (*Soldier*), Gilbert Servien (*Soldier*).

Filmed on locations in Paris, December 1962–January 1963. First shown in Paris, 31 May 1963; G.B., October 1964 (previously at London Film Festival, October 1963); U.S.A., 24 April 1968 (previously at New York Film Festival, 27 September 1967). Running time, 80 mins.
Distributors: Cocinor (France), Academy/Connoisseur (G.B.), West End Films (U.S.A.).
G.B. title: THE SOLDIERS.

Le Mépris (1963)

Production Company	Rome-Paris Films/Films Concordia (Paris)/ Compagnia Cinematografica Champion (Rome).
Producer	Georges de Beauregard, Carlo Ponti, Joseph E. Levine
Production Manager	Philippe Dussart, Carlo Lastricati
Director	Jean-Luc Godard
Assistant Director	Charles Bitsch
Script	Jean-Luc Godard. Based on the novel *Il Disprezzo* by Alberto Moravia
Director of Photography	Raoul Coutard (Franscope)
Colour Process	Technicolor
Editor	Agnès Guillemot, Lila Lakshmanan
Music	Georges Delerue (Italian version: Piero Piccioni)
Costumes	Janine Autre
Sound	William Sivel

Brigitte Bardot (*Camille Javal*), Michel Piccoli (*Paul Javal*), Jack Palance (*Jeremy Prokosch*), Fritz Lang (*Himself*), Giorgia Moll (*Francesca Vanini*), Jean-Luc Godard (*Assistant Director*), Linda Veras (*A Siren*).

Filmed on location in Rome and Capri (including Curzio Malaparte's villa), April–June 1963. First shown in Paris, 27 December 1963 (having been withdrawn from the Venice Film Festival by Joseph Levine); U.S.A., October 1964; G.B., at National Film Theatre, 3 November 1967. Running time, 100 mins. (France), 103 mins. (U.S.A.), 84 mins. (Italy).

Distributors: Marceau-Cocinor (France), Avco-Embassy (G.B.), Embassy (U.S.A.).

U.S. title: CONTEMPT; Italian title: IL DISPREZZO.

(Godard had his name removed from the credits of the Italian version because footage had been cut from *The Odyssey* sequence, the music and some dialogue altered, the colour changed, and certain sequences re-edited.)

Bande à Part (1964)

Production Company	Anouchka Films/Orsay Films (Paris)
Production Manager	Philippe Dussart
Director	Jean-Luc Godard
Assistant Director	Jean-Paul Savignac
Script	Jean-Luc Godard. Based on the novel *Fool's Gold* (*Pigeon Vole*) by Dolores Hitchens
Director of Photography	Raoul Coutard
Camera Operator	Georges Liron
Editor	Agnès Guillemot, Françoise Collin
Music	Michel Legrand
Sound	René Levert, Antoine Bonfanti
Narrator	Jean-Luc Godard

Anna Karina (*Odile*), Claude Brasseur (*Arthur*), Sami Frey (*Franz*), Louisa Colpeyn (*Madame Victoria*), Danièle Girard (*English Teacher*), Ernest Menzer (*Arthur's Uncle*), Chantal Darget (*Arthur's Aunt*), Michèle Seghers (*Pupil*), Claude Makovski (*Pupil*), Georges Staquet (*Légionnaire*), Michel Delahaye (*Doorman at language school*).

Filmed on location in Paris, February–March 1964. First shown at the Berlin Film Festival, 5 July 1964; Paris, 5 August 1964; G.B., November 1964 (previously at London Film Festival, November 1964); U.S.A., March 1966 (previously at New York Film Festival, September 1964). Running time, 95 mins.
Distributors: Columbia (France), Gala/Columbia (G.B.), Royal Films International (U.S.A.).
U.S. title: BAND OF OUTSIDERS; G.B. title: THE OUTSIDERS.

Une Femme Mariée (1964)

Production Company	Anouchka Films/Orsay Films (Paris)
Production Manager	Philippe Dussart
Director	Jean-Luc Godard
Assistant Director	Claude Othnin-Girard, Jean-Pierre Léaud, Hélène Kalouguine
Script	Jean-Luc Godard
Director of Photography	Raoul Coutard
Camera Operator	Georges Liron
Editor	Agnès Guillemot, Françoise Collin
Art Director	Henri Nogaret

Music	Extracts from Beethoven's Quartets nos. 7, 9, 10, 14, and 15
Jazz Music	Claude Nougaro
Song "Quand le film est triste"	J. D. Loudermilk, G. Aber, L. Morisse; sung by Sylvie Vartan
Sound	Antoine Bonfanti, René Levert, Jacques Maumont

Macha Méril (*Charlotte Giraud*), Bernard Noël (*Robert, the Lover*), Philippe Leroy (*Pierre, the Husband*), Roger Leenhardt (*Himself*), Rita Maiden (*Madame Céline*), Chris Tophe (*Nicolas*), Margaret Le-Van and Véronique Duval (*Two girls in swimming-pool bar*).

Filmed on location in Paris and at Orly Airport, June–July 1964. First shown at the Venice Film Festival (as *La Femme Mariée*), 8 September 1964; Paris (as *Une Femme Mariée*), 4 December 1964; G.B., April 1965; U.S.A., August 1965. Running time, 95 mins. (originally, 98 mins.). Distributors: Columbia (France), Gala/Columbia (G.B.), Royal Films International (U.S.A.).
U.S. title: THE MARRIED WOMAN; G.B. title: A MARRIED WOMAN. (The title change and minor cuts were imposed by the French Censor Board before the first Paris screening.)

Alphaville, Une Etrange Aventure de Lemmy Caution (1965)

Production Company	Chaumiane (Paris)/Filmstudio (Rome)
Producer	André Michelin
Production Manager	Philippe Dussart
Director	Jean-Luc Godard
Assistant Director	Charles Bitsch, Jean-Paul Savignac, Hélène Kalouguine
Script	Jean-Luc Godard
Director of Photography	Raoul Coutard
Camera Operator	Georges Liron
Editor	Agnès Guillemot
Music	Paul Misraki
Sound	René Levert

Eddie Constantine (*Lemmy Caution*), Anna Karina (*Natacha von Braun*), Akim Tamiroff (*Henri Dickson*), Howard Vernon (*Professor Léonard Nosfératu*, alias *von Braun*), Laszlo Szabo (*Chief Engineer*), Michel Delahaye (*von Braun's Assistant*), Jean-André Fieschi (*Professor Heckell*), Jean-Louis Comolli (*Professor Jeckell*).

Filmed on location in Paris, January–February 1965. First shown in Paris, 5 May 1965; U.S.A., October 1965 (previously at New York Film Festival, September 1965); G.B., March 1966 (previously at London Film Festival, November 1965). Running time, 98 mins.
Distributors: Athos (France), Academy/Connoisseur (G.B.), Pathé Contemporary (U.S.A.).

Pierrot le Fou (1965)

Production Company	Rome-Paris Films (Paris)/Dino de Laurentiis Cinematografica (Rome)
Producer	Georges de Beauregard
Production Manager	René Demoulin
Director	Jean-Luc Godard
Assistant Director	Philippe Fourastié, Jean-Pierre Léaud
Script	Jean-Luc Godard. Based on the novel *Obsession* by Lionel White
Director of Photography	Raoul Coutard (Techniscope)
Colour Process	Eastman Colour
Camera Operator	Georges Liron
Editor	Françoise Collin
Art Director	Pierre Guffroy
Music	Antoine Duhamel
Songs "Ma Ligne de Chance" and "Jamais je ne t'ai dit que je t'aimerai toujours"	Antoine Duhamel, Bassiak
Sound	René Levert

Jean-Paul Belmondo (*Ferdinand*), Anna Karina (*Marianne*), Dirk Sanders (*Marianne's Brother*), Raymond Devos (*The Man on the pier*), Graziella Galvani (*Ferdinand's Wife*), Roger Dutoit (*Gangster*), Hans Meyer (*Gangster*), Jimmy Karoubi (*Dwarf*), Christa Nell (*Mme. Staquet*), Pascal Aubier (*2nd Brother*), Pierre Hanin (*3rd Brother*), Princess Aicha Abidir (*Herself*), Samuel Fuller (*Himself*), Alexis Poliakoff (*Sailor*), Laszlo Szabo (*Political Exile from Santo Domingo*), Jean-Pierre Léaud (*Young Man in cinema*).

Filmed on location in Paris and the South of France, June–July 1965. First shown at the Venice Film Festival, 29 August 1965; Paris, 5 November 1965; G.B., April 1966 (previously at London Film Festival, November 1965); U.S.A. (New York Film Festival, September 1966). Running time, 110 mins.
Distributors: S.N.C. Impérial (France), Gala (G.B.).

Masculin Féminin (1966)

Production Company	Anouchka Films/Argos-Films (Paris)/ Svensk Filmindustri/Sandrews (Stockholm)
Production Manager	Philippe Dussart
Director	Jean-Luc Godard
Assistant Director	Bernard Toublanc-Michel, Jacques Barratier
Script	Jean-Luc Godard. Based on two stories, *La Femme de Paul* and *Le Signe* by Guy de Maupassant
Director of Photography	Willy Kurant
Editor	Agnès Guillemot
Music	Francis Lai
Sound	René Levert

Jean-Pierre Léaud (*Paul*), Chantal Goya (*Madeleine*), Catherine-Isabelle Duport (*Catherine*), Marlène Jobert (*Elizabeth*), Michel Debord (*Robert*), Birger Malmsten (*The Man in film-within-the-film*), Eva Britt Strandberg (*The Woman in film-within-the-film*), Brigitte Bardot and Antoine Bourseiller (*Couple rehearsing play in café*), Chantal Darget (*Woman in Métro*), Elsa Leroy ("*Mademoiselle 19 ans*"), Françoise Hardy (*Friend of American Officer in car*).

Filmed on location in Paris, November–December 1965. First shown in Paris, 22 April 1966; G.B., June 1967; U.S.A., October 1966 (previously at New York Film Festival, September 1966). Running time, 110 mins. (103 mins. in U.S.A.). Distributors: Columbia (France), Gala (G.B.), Royal Films International (U.S.A.).

Made in U.S.A. (1966)

Production Company	Rome-Paris Films/Anouchka Films/ S.E.P.I.C. (Paris)
Producer	Georges de Beauregard
Production Manager	René Demoulin
Director	Jean-Luc Godard
Assistant Director	Charles Bitsch, Claude Bakka, Jean-Pierre Léaud, Philippe Pouzenc
Script	Jean-Luc Godard. Based on the novel *Rien dans le coffre* by Richard Stark
Director of Photography	Raoul Coutard (Techniscope)

Colour Process	Eastman Colour
Camera Operator	Georges Liron
Editor	Agnès Guillemot
Music	Beethoven, Schumann
Sound	René Levert, Jacques Maumont

Anna Karina (*Paula Nelson*), Laszlo Szabo (*Richard Widmark*), Jean-Pierre Léaud (*Donald Siegel*), Yves Alfonso (*David Goodis*), Ernest Menzer (*Edgar Typhus*), Jean-Claude Bouillon (*Inspector Aldrich*), Kyoko Kosaka (*Doris Mizoguchi*), Marianne Faithfull (*Herself*), Claude Bakka (*Man with Marianne Faithfull*), Philippe Labro (*Himself*), Rémo Forlani (*Workman in bar*), Marc Dudicourt (*Barman*), Jean-Pierre Biesse (*Richard Nixon*), Sylvain Godet (*Robert MacNamara*), Alexis Poliakoff (*Man with notebook and red telephone*), Eliane Giovagnoli (*Dentist's Assistant*), Roger Scipion (*Dr. Korvo*), Danièle Palmero (*Hotel Chambermaid*), Rita Maiden (*Woman who gives Paula information*), Isabelle Pons (*Provincial Journalist*), Philippe Pouzenc (*Policeman*), Fernand Coquet (*Billposter*), Miguel (*Dentist*), Annie Guégan (*Girl in bandages*), Marika Perioli (*Girl with dog*), Jean-Philippe Nierman (*Note-taking policeman*), Charles Bitsch (*Taxi-driver*), Daniel Bart (*Policeman*), and Jean-Luc Godard (*Voice of Richard Politzer*).

Filmed on location in Paris, July–August 1966. First shown at the London Film Festival, 3 December 1966; Paris, 27 January 1967; U.S.A., New York Film Festival, 27 September 1967. Running time, 90 mins. Distributors: Lux (France).

Deux ou Trois Choses que je sais d'elle (1966)

Production Company	Anouchka Films/Argos-Films/Les Films du Carrosse/Parc Film (Paris)
Production Manager	Philippe Senné
Director	Jean-Luc Godard
Assistant Director	Charles Bitsch, Isabelle Pons
Script	Jean-Luc Godard. Suggested by an inquiry by Catherine Vimenet published in *Le Nouvel Observateur*
Director of Photography	Raoul Coutard (Techniscope)
Colour Process	Eastman Colour
Camera Operator	Georges Liron
Editor	Françoise Collin, Chantal Delattre

Music	Beethoven
Sound	René Levert, Antoine Bonfanti
Narrator	Jean-Luc Godard

Marina Vlady (*Juliette Janson*), Anny Duperey (*Marianne*), Roger Mont-soret (*Robert Janson*), Jean Narboni (*Roger*), Christophe Bourseiller (*Christophe*), Marie Bourseiller (*Solange*), Raoul Lévy (*John Bogus*), Joseph Gehrard (*Monsieur Gérard*), Helena Bielicic (*Girl in Bath*), Robert Chevassu (*Electricity Meter-reader*), Yves Beneyton (*Long-haired Youth*), Jean-Pierre Laverne (*The Writer*), Blandine Jeanson (*The Student*), Claude Miler (*Bouvard*), Jean-Patrick Lebel (*Pécuchet*), Juliet Berto (*Girl who talks to Robert*), Anna Manga (*Woman in Basement*), Benjamin Rosette (*Man in Basement*), Helen Scott (*Woman at pin-ball machine*).

Filmed on locations in Paris, August–September 1966. First shown in Paris, 17 March 1967; G.B. (London Film Festival, 24 November 1967); U.S.A. (New York Film Festival, 25 September 1968). Running time, 95 mins.
Distributor: U.G.C./Sirius/C.F.D.C. (France).

La Chinoise, ou plutôt à la Chinoise (1967)

Production Company	Productions de la Guéville/Parc Films/ Simar Films/Anouchka Films/Athos-Films
Production Manager	Philippe Dussart
Director	Jean-Luc Godard
Assistant Director	Charles Bitsch
Script	Jean-Luc Godard
Director of Photography	Raoul Coutard
Colour Process	Eastman Colour
Camera Operator	Georges Liron
Editor	Agnès Guillemot, Delphine Desfons
Music	Karl-Heinz Stockhausen
Sound	René Levert

Anne Wiazemsky (*Véronique*), Jean-Pierre Léaud (*Guillaume*), Michel Sémeniako (*Henri*), Lex de Bruïjn (*Kirilov*), Juliet Berto (*Yvonne*), Omar Diop (*Comrade X*), Francis Jeanson.

Filmed on locations in Paris, March 1967. First shown in Paris, 30 August 1967; G.B. (London Film Festival, 24 November 1967); U.S.A., April 1968. Running time, 90 mins.
Distributors: Athos (France), Leacock-Pennebaker Films (U.S.A.).

Loin du Viêt-nam (1967)

Production Company	Slon
Directors	Alain Resnais, William Klein, Joris Ivens, Agnès Varda [episode not included], Claude Lelouch, Jean-Luc Godard
Organisers	Jacqueline Meppiel, Andrea Haran
Principal Collaborators	Michèle Ray, Roger Pic, K. S. Karol, Marceline Loridan, François Maspero, Chris Marker, Jacques Sternberg, Jean Lacoutre, Willy Kurant, Jean Bosty, Kieu Tham, Denis Clairval, Ghislain Cloquet, Bernard Zitzerman, Alain Levent, Théo Robichet, Antoine Bonfanti, Harold Maury, Claire Grunstein, Alain Franchet, Didier Beaudet, Florence Malraux, Marie-Louise Guinet, Roger de Menestrol, Ragnar, Jean Ravel, Colette Leloup, Eric Pluet, Albert Jurgenson, Ethel Blum, Michèle Bouder, Christian Quinson, Jean Larivière, Maurice Carrel, Bernard Fresson, Karen Blanguernon, Anne Bellec, Valérie Mayoux
Colour Process	Eastman Colour (in part only)
Uncredited Supervisory Editor	Chris Marker

Compiled from footage shot in the U.S.A., Vietnam, Cuba and France. First shown at the Montreal Film Festival, August 1967; U.S.A., 6 June 1968 (previously at New York Film Festival, 30 September 1967); Paris, 13 December 1967 (previously at Besançon before an audience of Trade Union members, 18 October 1967); G.B., 28 December 1967 (previously at London Film Festival, 29 November 1967). Running time, 115 mins.
Distributors: Films 13 (France), Contemporary (G.B.), New Yorker Films (U.S.A.).
U.S./G.B. title: FAR FROM VIETNAM.

184

Week-end (1967)

Production Company	Comacico/Les Films Copernic/Lira Films (Paris)/Ascot Cineraid (Rome)
Production Manager	Ralph Baum, Philippe Senné
Director	Jean-Luc Godard
Assistant Director	Claude Miler
Script	Jean-Luc Godard
Director of Photography	Raoul Coutard
Colour Process	Eastman Colour
Editor	Agnès Guillemot
Music	Antoine Duhamel; Mozart's piano sonata K 576
Song "Allo, tu m'entends"	Guy Béart
Sound	René Levert

Mireille Darc (*Corinne*), Jean Yanne (*Roland*), Jean-Pierre Kalfon (*Leader of the F.L.S.O.*), Valérie Lagrange (*His Moll*), Jean-Pierre Léaud (*Saint-Just/Man in Phone Booth*), Yves Beneyton (*Member of the F.L.S.O.*), Paul Gégauff (*Pianist*), Daniel Pommereulle (*Joseph Balsamo*), Yves Afonso (*Gros Poucet*), Blandine Jeanson (*Emily Bronte/Girl in Farmyard*), Ernest Menzer (*Cook*), Georges Staquet (*Tractor Driver*), Juliet Berto (*Girl in Car Crash/Member of the F.L.S.O.*), Anne Wiazemsky (*Girl in Farmyard/ Member of the F.L.S.O.*), Virginie Vignon (*Marie-Madeleine*), Monsieur Jojot, Isabelle Pons.

Filmed on location in the Paris region, September–October 1967. First shown in Paris, 29 December 1967; G.B., 5 July 1968; U.S.A., 30 September 1968 (previously at New York Film Festival, 27 September 1968). Running time, 95 mins.
Distributors: Athos (France), Connoisseur (G.B.), Grove Press (U.S.A.).

Le Gai Savoir (1968)

Production Company	Anouchka Films (Paris)/Bavaria Atelier (Munich)
Director	Jean-Luc Godard
Script	Jean-Luc Godard
Director of Photography	Jean Leclerc
Colour Process	Eastman Colour

Juliet Berto (*Patricia*), Jean-Pierre Léaud (*Emile Rousseau*).

Filmed at the Joinville Studios, December 1967–January 1968 for the O.R.T.F., who subsequently refused to show it and eventually sold the

rights back to Godard. First shown at the Berlin Film Festival, 28 June 1969; G.B., 12 July 1969; U.S.A. (New York Film Festival, 27 September 1969). Running time, 91 mins.
Distributor: Kestrel Productions (G.B.), Leacock-Pennebaker Films (U.S.A.).

Un Film Comme Les Autres (1968)

Filmed in 16 mm., presumably during May–June 1968. Running time, 120 mins. No information is available about this film, which has had a public screening early in 1969 at the Philharmonic Hall in New York.
Distributor: Leacock-Pennebaker Films (U.S.A.).

One Plus One (1968)

Production Company	Cupid Productions
Executive Producer	Eleni Collard
Producer	Michael Pearson, Iain Quarrier
Production Manager	Clive Freedman, Paul de Burgh
Director	Jean-Luc Godard
Script	Jean-Luc Godard
Director of Photography	Tony Richmond
Colour Process	Eastman Colour
Camera Operator	Colin Corby
Editor	Ken Rowles
Music	The Rolling Stones
Sound	Arthur Bradburn
Narrator	Sean Lynch

The Rolling Stones [Mick Jagger, Keith Richard, Brian Jones, Charlie Watts, Bill Wyman], Anne Wiazemsky, Iain Quarrier, Frankie Dymon, Jnr., Danny Daniels, Illario Pedro, Roy Stewart, Limbert Spencer, Tommy Ansar, Michael McKay, Rudi Patterson, Mark Matthew, Karl Lewis, Bernard Boston, Niké Arrighi, Françoise Pascal, Joanna David, Monica Walters, Glenna Forster Jones, Elizabeth Long, Jeanette Wild, Harry Douglas, Colin Cunningham, Graham Peet, Matthew Knox, Barbara Coleridge.

Filmed on locations in London, at the Olympic Recording Studios, Barnes, and at Camber Sands, Sussex, June–August 1968 (with interruptions). First shown at the London Film Festival, 29 November 1968; Paris, 9 May 1969. Running time, 99 mins.
Distributors: Images (France), Connoisseur (G.B.).
Alternative title: SYMPATHY FOR THE DEVIL.

One American Movie/1 A.M. (1968/69)

Production Company	Leacock-Pennebaker, Inc.
Director	Jean-Luc Godard
Script	Jean-Luc Godard
Director of Photography	D. A. Pennebaker, Richard Leacock

Rip Torn, The Jefferson Airplane, Eldridge Cleaver, Tom Hayden, Le Roi Jones.

Filmed in colour on locations in New York, New Jersey, and Berkeley, California, autumn 1968. Still uncompleted.

British Sounds (1969)

Production Company	Kestrel Productions (for London Weekend Television)
Producer	Irving Teitelbaum, Kenith Trodd
Director	Jean-Luc Godard
Script	Jean-Luc Godard
Director of Photography	Charles Stewart
Colour Process	Eastman Colour
Editor	Elizabeth Kozmian
Sound	Fred Sharp
Researcher	Mo Teitelbaum

Filmed in 16 mm. on locations in England, at the BMC plant at Abingdon and at the University of Essex, February 1969. Running time, 52 mins.

Le Vent d'Est (1969)

Production Company	CCC (Berlin)/Poli Film (Rome)/Anouchka Films (Paris)
Director	Jean-Luc Godard
Script	Daniel Cohn-Bendit
Director of Photography	Mario Vulpiano
Colour Process	Eastman Colour

Gian Maria Volonté (*Soldier*), Anne Wiazemsky (*Whore*), Daniel Cohn-Bendit, George Götz, Christian Tullio, Marco Ferreri.

Filmed on locations in Italy, on the Western town set at Elios Studios, and the soundstages at De Paolis Studios, May 1969.

Shorts

Opération Béton (1954)

Production Company	Actua Film (Geneva)
Producer ⎫	
Director ⎬	Jean-Luc Godard
Script ⎭	
Director of Photography	Adrien Porchet
Editor	Jean-Luc Godard
Music	Handel, Bach

Filmed on location at La Grande-Dixence, Switzerland. Running time, 20 mins.
Distributor: Gaumont (France).

Une Femme Coquette (1955)

Production Company	Jean-Luc Godard (Geneva)
Producer ⎫	Jean-Luc Godard
Director ⎭	
Script	Hans Lucas (i.e. Jean-Luc Godard). Based on the story *Le Signe* by Guy de Maupassant
Director of Photography ⎫	Hans Lucas (i.e. J.-L. G.)
Editor ⎭	
Music	Bach

Maria Lysandre (*The Woman*), Roland Tolma (*The Man*), Jean-Luc Godard (*The Client*).

Filmed on location in 16 mm. in Geneva. Running time, 10 mins.

Tous les Garçons s'appellent Patrick (1957)

Production Company	Les Films de la Pléiade (Paris)
Producer	Pierre Braunberger
Director	Jean-Luc Godard
Script	Eric Rohmer
Director of Photography	Michel Latouche
Editor	Cécile Decugis
Music	Beethoven
Sound	Jacques Maumont

Jean-Claude Brialy (*Patrick*), Nicole Berger (*Véronique*), Anne Colette (*Charlotte*).

Filmed on location in Paris. Running time, 21 mins.
Distributors: Gaumont (France), Connoisseur (G.B.).
Alternative French title: CHARLOTTE ET VERONIQUE; G.B. title: ALL BOYS ARE CALLED PATRICK.

Charlotte et son Jules (1958)

Production Company	Les Films de la Pléiade (Paris)
Producer	Pierre Braunberger
Director	Jean-Luc Godard
Script	Jean-Luc Godard
Director of Photography	Michel Latouche
Editor	Jean-Luc Godard
Music	Pierre Monsigny
Sound	Jacques Maumont

Jean-Paul Belmondo [voice dubbed by Jean-Luc Godard] (*Jean*), Anne Colette (*Charlotte*), Gérard Blain (*Charlotte's Friend*).

Filmed in Godard's hotel room, Rue de Rennes, Paris. Running time, 20 mins. (14 mins. in G.B.).
Distributors: Unidex (France), Connoisseur (G.B.).

Une Histoire d'Eau (1958)

Production Company	Les Films de la Pléiade (Paris)
Producer	Pierre Braunberger
Production Manager	Roger Fleytoux
Director	François Truffaut, Jean-Luc Godard
Script	Jean-Luc Godard
Director of Photography	Michel Latouche
Editor	Jean-Luc Godard
Sound	Jacques Maumont
Narrator	Jean-Luc Godard

Jean-Claude Brialy (*The Young Man*), Caroline Dim (*The Girl*).

Filmed on location in Paris by Truffaut, completed by Godard. Running time, 20 mins. (12 mins. in G.B.).
Distributors: Unidex (France), Connoisseur (G.B.).

Sketches

La Paresse (sketch in *Les Sept Péchés Capitaux*) (1961)

Production Company	Films Gibé/Franco-London Films (Paris)/ Titanus (Rome)
Production Manager	Jean Lavie
Director	Jean-Luc Godard
Assistant Director	Marin Karmitz
Script	Jean-Luc Godard
Director of Photography	Henri Decaë (Dyaliscope)
Camera Operator	Jean-Paul Schwartz
Editor	Jacques Gaillard
Music	Michel Legrand
Sound	Jean-Claude Marchetti, Jean Labussière

Eddie Constantine (*Himself*), Nicole Mirel (*The Starlet*).

Filmed on location in Paris, September 1961. First shown in Paris, 7 March 1962; U.S.A., November 1962; G.B. (at National Film Theatre, June 1966).
Distributors: Consortium Pathé (France), Embassy (U.S.A.).
U.S. title: SLOTH in THE SEVEN CAPITAL SINS.

Le Nouveau Monde (sketch in *RoGoPaG*) (1962)

Production Company	Arco Film/Cineriz (Rome)/Lyre Film (Paris)
Producer	Alfredo Bini
Production Manager	Yves Laplache
Director	Jean-Luc Godard
Script	Jean-Luc Godard
Director of Photography	Jean Rabier
Editor	Agnès Guillemot, Lila Lakshmanan
Music	Beethoven
Sound	Hervé

Alexandra Stewart (*Alexandra*), Jean-Marc Bory (*The Narrator*), Jean-André Fieschi, Michel Delahaye.

Filmed on location in Paris, November 1962. First shown in Italy, March 1963; U.S.A. (New York Film Festival, September 1963); G.B. (London Film Festival, October 1963). Running time of sketch, 20 mins.
Distributors: Cineriz (Italy).
(Banned ten days after opening in Italy, *Rogopag* was subsequently passed with cuts under the title of *Laviamoci il Cervello*. The Italian title of Godard's sketch is *Il Nuovo Mondo*.)

Le Grand Escroc (sketch for *Les Plus Belles Escroqueries du Monde*) (1963)

Production Company	Ulysse Productions (Paris)/Primex Films (Marseille)/Vides (Rome)/Toho (Tokyo)/ Caesar Film (Amsterdam)
Producer	Pierre Roustang
Production Manager	Philippe Dussart
Director	Jean-Luc Godard
Assistant Director	Charles Bitsch
Script	Jean-Luc Godard
Director of Photography	Raoul Coutard (Franscope)
Editor	Agnès Guillemot, Lila Lakshmanan
Music	Michel Legrand
Sound	Hervé
Narrator	Jean-Luc Godard

Jean Seberg (*Patricia Leacock*), Charles Denner (*The Swindler*), Laszlo Szabo (*Police Inspector*).

Filmed on location in Marrakesh, January 1963. Godard's sketch was cut from the film when it was first shown in Paris, August 1964. First shown (separately) at the London Film Festival, 24 November 1967. Running time of sketch, 20 mins. Distributors: Lux (France).

Montparnasse-Levallois (sketch in *Paris vu par . . .*) (1963)

Production Company	Films du Losange/Barbet Schroeder (Paris)
Producer	Barbet Schroeder
Associate Producer	Patrick Bauchau
Director	Jean-Luc Godard
Script	Jean-Luc Godard
Director of Photography	Albert Maysles
Colour Process	Ektachrome: Eastman Colour print
Editor	Jacqueline Raynal
Sound	René Levert

Johanna Shimkus (*Monika*), Philippe Hiquilly (*Ivan*), Serge Davri (*Roger*).

Filmed on location (in 16 mm., later blown up to 35 mm.), in Paris, December 1963. First shown at the Cannes Film Festival, 19 May 1965; Paris, October 1965; U.S.A. (New York Film Festival, September 1965); G.B., February 1966 (previously at London Film Festival, November 1965). Running time of sketch, 12 mins.
Distributors: Sodireg (France), Amanda (G.B.).
G.B. title: SIX IN PARIS.

Anticipation, ou L'An 2,000 (sketch in *Le Plus Vieux Métier du Monde ou L'Amour à travers les Ages*) (1967)

Production Company	Francoriz Films/Les Films Gibé (Paris)/ Rialto Films (Berlin)/Rizzoli Films (Rome)
Producer	Joseph Bergholz
Director	Jean-Luc Godard
Assistant Director	Charles Bitsch
Script	Jean-Luc Godard
Director of Photography	Pierre Lhomme
Colour Process	Eastman Colour
Editor	Agnès Guillemot
Music	Michel Legrand

Jacques Charrier (*John Dmitrios*), Marilù Tolo (*1st Prostitute—Physical Love*), Anna Karina (*Eléonor Roméovitch—Sentimental Love*), Jean-Pierre Léaud (*Bellboy*), Daniel Bart, Jean-Patrick Lebel.

Filmed on location in Paris and Orly Airport, November 1966. First shown in Paris, 21 April 1967; G.B., 20 October 1967. Distributors: Athos (France), Miracle (G.B.).

L'Enfant Prodigue (sketch in *Vangelo '70*) (1967)

Production Company	Castoro Film (Rome)/Anouchka Films (Paris)
Director	Jean-Luc Godard
Assistant Director	Charles Bitsch
Script	Jean-Luc Godard
Director of Photography	Alain Levent
Editor	Agnès Guillemot
Music	Giovanni Fusco
Sound	Guy Villette

Christine Guého (*Her*), Catherine Jourdan (*Female Witness*), Nino Castelnuovo (*Him*), Paolo Pozzesi (*Male Witness*).

First shown at the London Film Festival, 24 November 1967. Running time of sketch, 26 mins.

Acknowledgements

The author would like to thank Tom Milne and Jan Dawson who did the Filmography; Cedric Pheasant who made the frame enlargements; Pamela Balfry, Margaret Turner, and Sylvia Loeb who did the typing; Yvonne Goldstein and Pierre Rissient, and J.-L. G. who arranged screenings and re-screenings; Hilary and Mary Evans, Jean Yves Mock, and David Wilson who read and re-read and made many helpful suggestions; finally, Penelope Houston, without whom . . .